88 Hints for GROWING GARDEN FLOWERS

88 Hints for GROWING GARDEN FLOWERS

By Radoslav Šrot

SUNBURST BOOKS

Designed and produced by Aventinum

English language edition first published 1994
by Sunburst Books, 65 Old Church Street, London SW3 5BS

Text by Radoslav Šrot
Translated by Elizabeth Kindlová
Illustrations by Miloš Váňa, Radoslava Vodáková and Vlastimil Vodák
Photographs by Radoslav Šrot, Helena Atanasová, Vladimír Havelka,
Vladimír Plicka, Vladimír Pokorný, Josef Ptáček, Rudolf Schulák, Vlastimil Vaněk
and Libuše Zadníčková
Graphic design by Stanislav Seifert

ISBN 1 85778 109 0
Printed in the Czech Republic
3/22/03/51-01

Introduction

Growing flowers is the most effective way to brighten up your garden and keep it looking attractive from spring right through to winter. No matter how small the area which is available, it is possible to grow a range of plant species and varieties, and to create an impressive array of colours, shapes and textures.

All that it takes is some forethought and imagination to transform flowerbeds into a more or less perpetual display of perennials, annuals and biennials. The individual clumps of flowers can be exchanged for others as desired, in order to maintain a constantly changing splash of colour.

In addition, if sufficient space is available, ornamental garden elements can be incorporated into your display to provide a setting which enhances the flowers of your choice. For example, a rockery, dry wall, pergola or ornamental pool.

Once you have started constructing your ideal garden, you will find that the opportunities are endless, and that this satisfying hobby presents enormous scope for creativity, enjoyment and relaxation.

This book presents a comprehensive yet concise guide to growing garden flowers for the aspiring gardener. The information provided about each species of flower includes details on the ideal environmental conditions, as well as advice on planting, feeding, protection and propagation. These thoroughly practical, helpful hints will be the basis of your success in growing garden flowers.

Contents

1 Basic Plant Needs: Light and Warmth

Most flowering plants grow best on a sunny site ○; direct sunlight enables them to grow well, produce abundant flowers, and resist disease. Many other species prefer a semi-shaded site ◑, under tall trees, for instance, or in a place that is shaded during the hottest time of the day by other plants or buildings. In the direct noon-day sun of summer such plants would suffer from lack of moisture. Considerably fewer flowering plants require a shady site ●, but they also include some very attractive species. The symbols shown here indicate the plants' requirements of heat and light; they commonly appear on plant and seed packets and provide a useful indication of where the plants should be sited in the garden.

—

Plants are, however, fairly flexible in their demands on light. Many sun-loving species grow quite happily on semi-shaded sites, though they may not develop such a rich display of flowers as those in direct sunlight. Again, many semi-shade species also grow well in sunny sites provided there is enough moisture in the soil. However, shade-loving plants — particularly those with more delicate leaves — lose their fresh leaf colour in direct sunlight and the leaves may suffer brownish burn spots. Plants that are grouped too close together suffer from inadequate light. As a result, photosynthesis — the process by which a plant uses the energy in sunlight to produce the foods it needs for growth — is reduced, resulting in most cases in stunted, unhealthy plants liable to be attacked by diseases and pests.

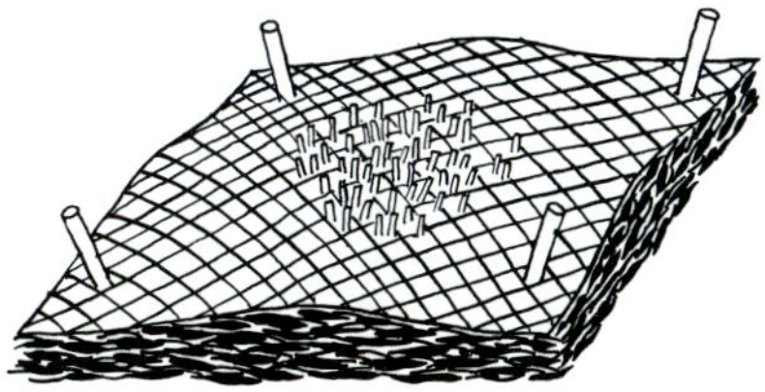

Protect perennials which cannot tolerate sharp winter frosts with a 5—10 cm (2—4 in) thick cover of leaves or other mulch; if exposed to winds, cover the leaves with a wire mesh or conifer branches.

Too much sunlight in winter may damage evergreen plants which are normally resistant to frost. Sunlight stimulates a plant to evaporate water vapour through its foliage. Normally, this loss of moisture is made good by drawing water up through the roots. But if the soil is frozen to any depth, the plant cannot replace the loss, and if the soil remains frozen for a long time, the plant may die. It is often mistakenly assumed that such a plant has frozen to death. In fact, it has died of thirst.

●

Plants from warmer countries suffer from low temperatures at the beginning of the growing period as well as in winter. For this reason their seedlings are not planted out in the garden until the last spring frosts have gone — usually in late May. This applies to many popular annuals, such as fibrous-rooted begonias, marigolds (*Tagetes*), mesembryanthemum or Livingstone daisy (*Dorotheanthus*) and floss flower (*Ageratum*) as well as half-hardy tuberous perennials which are planted as pre-cultivated seedlings. If there is a danger that the tubers or bulbs of plants such as gladioli may freeze in the soil in winter, they must be dug up in the autumn and stored in a frost-free place. The roots of perennials sensitive to winter frost — for instance, pampas grass (*Cortaderia selloana*) and Japanese anemone (*Anemone* x *hybrida*) — should be protected by a cover of leaves or straw. The more robust species, however, may be damaged if covered up because, if there is a sudden thaw at the end of winter, they could rot owing to the absence of air beneath the cover. However, in extremely frosty winter weather, and particularly if there is no snow on the ground, a temporary thermal cover helps even the hardiest plants.

Hellebores (*Helleborus*) grow well on a sheltered, semi-shaded or shaded site.

2 Plants and the Soil

In general, most plants will grow satisfactorily in medium-heavy soils that contain adequate amounts of humus, nutrients and moisture. These soils, which are clayey or sandy-clayey with a good structure, are adequately aerated and so contain sufficient oxygen for the roots of plants and soil micro-organisms which, by their actions, make the soil fertile. After rain or flooding, medium-heavy soils retain the required amount of water for plants, while the surplus drains away downwards. These soils are easy to work with garden tools. In order to maintain their fertility, their humus and nutrient content must be increased regularly. The best way to do this is to use good garden compost. Peat and well-rotted farmyard manure, dug into the soil at a concentration of 3—4 kg (6.5—9 lb) to the square metre every three years, will help to improve its structure.

Most flowering plants do not thrive in heavy clayey soils, which are badly aerated and do not absorb water well. After long rains they become waterlogged, while in prolonged dry spells they harden and are difficult to cultivate. In order to improve it, heavy clay must be aerated and its porosity increased by working a bucketfull of coarse sand into each square metre. If need be, this process can be repeated after several years. The humus content is increased by regularly adding garden compost

◄ 'Russell Lupins', the most popular of the strains of *Lupinus* perennials, thrive in acid or neutral soils in sun or partial shade.

or neutralized peat. It is also important to add lime (ground limestone, chalk, or hydrated lime) to heavy soil every 3—4 years. This will reduce the soil's acidity and so enable soil bacteria to become more active.

Sandy soils, in contrast, are too aerated and porous. They cannot retain sufficient moisture, which drains away into the subsoil, carrying with it many of the soil's nutrients. To improve these soils, dig in plenty of bulky organic material such as well-rotted garden compost or farmyard manure, together with heavier garden soil. You can also apply a mulch — a layer of peat, leaf-mould or composted bark — to the soil surface before it dries out. A dark-coloured mulch will also help the soil to retain heat. Stony, flinty soils should be treated in the same way. If the soil is exceptionally stony, you will need to dig out most of the stones to a depth of at least 30 cm (12 in) before improving the soil's structure.

If your soil suffers from long-term waterlogging, this may be caused by a layer of impermeable soil, called a hardpan, underlying the topsoil at a depth of about 15—25 cm (6—10 in) below the surface. The problem may be cured by breaking up the hardpan. If waterlogging continues, however, you may have to lay land drains.

Tools for working the soil: (1) hoeing fork; (2) narrow pointed spade; (3) hoe; (4) metal rake, (5) small weeding frame; (6) small hand hoe; (7) hand cultivator; (8) planting trowel; (9) weed-extractor; (10) potted seedling and bulb planter.

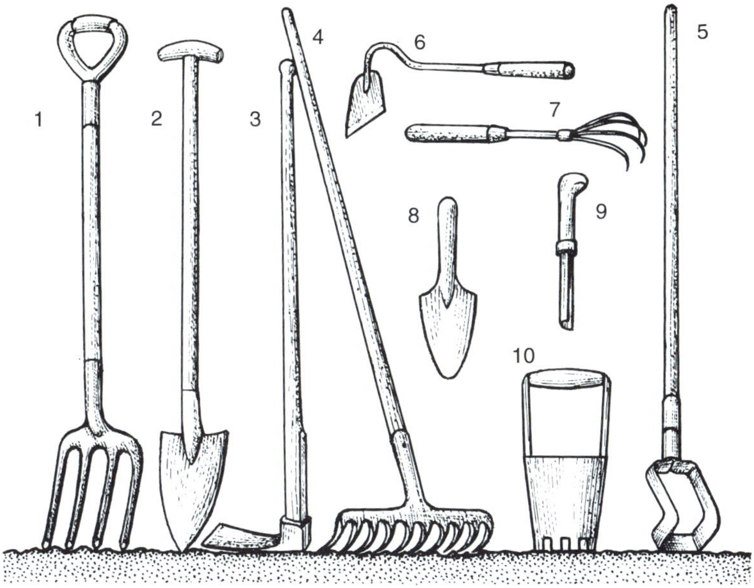

3 Soil Types and How to Modify Them

Chemically-speaking, soils are acid or alkaline or neutral. As some flowering plants (rhododendrons, camellias, heaths and heathers, for instance) grow only in acid soil, while others prefer alkaline or neutral soil, it is important to know which type of soil is in your garden before you plan your planting programme. Soil acidity or alkalinity is defined by a logarithmic system known as the *p*H scale, which ranges from 0 to 14. A *p*H of 7.0 is neutral, above 7.0 is increasingly alkaline, while below 7.0 is increasingly acid. A *p*H of 5.0 is ten times as acid as *p*H 6.0; a *p*H of 9.0 is ten times as alkaline as *p*H 8.0.

●

The *p*H of your soil can be measured with one of the many inexpensive soil-testing kits available from garden centres and horticultural stores. The kits include an indicator solution which you mix in a test tube with soil samples from your garden. The solution will turn a certain colour depending on the acidity or otherwise of the mixture, and this can be compared with the colours on a chart supplied with the kit.

◀ Most heaths and heathers, such as this Cornish heath (*Erica vagans*), prefer acid soil.

Most species of flowering plants grow best in soil which is either neutral or very slightly acid (*p*H 6.8 to 6.5). Acid-loving plants, apart from those already mentioned, include those species that grow best in shady or damp conditions, while many plants that like a dryish soil in full sunlight prefer an alkaline soil.

Iris cultivars (*Iris* x *barbata*) require calcium in the soil.

●

Within limits — that is, in a fairly small area of a flower bed or border — you can modify the *p*H of your soil to suit a particular choice of plants. An acid soil with a *p*H of 5.5 or less can be made more alkaline by adding fine limestone or chalk at a rate of 200 g (7 oz) per square metre.

●

Because most soils have a tendency to become increasingly acid over a period of time, many gardeners routinely add lime to their soil every few years. For liming the soil around individual plants such as irises or primroses at an early stage of growth, finely ground egg-shells can be used. For plants which love acid soil, alkaline and neutral soils can be treated with sulphate of ammonia and sulphate of potash, two of the acid-reacting fertilizers. The structure of acid soils can be improved, without raising their alkalinity, by digging in acid sphagnum peat.

Use litmus papers to discover whether the soil is acid or alkaline.

4 Basic Plant Needs: Water

The amount of water flowering plants require varies greatly from species to species. Whereas the needs of plants that like dry, well-drained soil are normally satisfied by natural rainfall, or occasional watering during a period of exceptionally dry weather, most species require more frequent watering, while moisture-loving plants must be grown on a site with a constant surplus of water in the soil. And then, of course, the plants that furnish your ornamental pond live all their lives in water.

●

Flowering plants require a greater amount of water in spring during their stage of most intensive growth. In an abnormally dry spring the soil has insufficient moisture and the plants must be given regular and substantial watering — just as in the hot, dry spells of summer.

Apart from the soil water which they take up through their roots, some flowering plants need a humid atmosphere to do their best. The herbaceous perennial *Phlox paniculata,* for instance, grows best in foothill regions where the air is damper. Greater air moisture is also required when propagating plants from herbaceous cuttings in a frame. On the other hand, if the atmosphere is too moist, some plants suffer from fungal diseases such as mildew — typical victims being the Michaelmas daisies (*Aster* ssp.) — and leaf blackspot, which is particularly severe on florist's chrysanthemums (varieties of *C. indicum*).

•

Some perennials cannot tolerate wet soil during their dormant period and their roots often rot. Most such vulnerable species are natives of dry steppes or mountains, where the ground in winter is covered by a thick carpet of snow but the underlying topsoil may not become sodden until the spring thaw. Such plants need to be carefully sited in the garden. In winter they should be protected from the rain or snow by an impervious cover. Or they can be planted on a slight slope, so that surplus water will drain away. In a rockery those plants sensitive to winter moisture or to low temperatures can be grown in flower-pots and transferred to an unheated greenhouse after the end of the growing season.

Protect pampas grass (*Cortaderia selloana*) against sharp frosts and the coldest winter winds by placing a sack filled with dry leaves or crushed polystyrene over it.

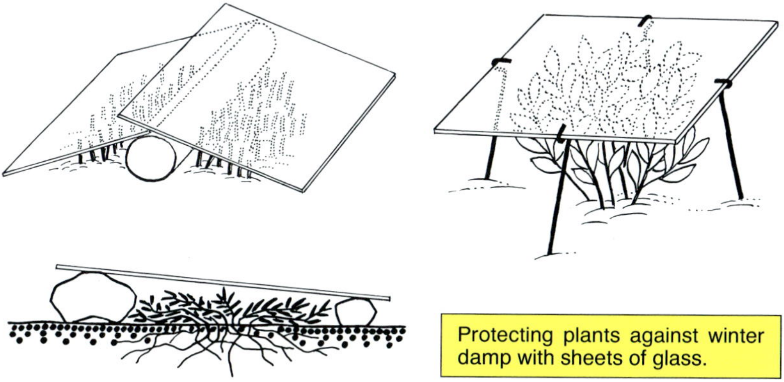

Protecting plants against winter damp with sheets of glass.

5 Watering Your Plants: When and How

Until recently it was generally accepted that rainwater was the most suitable water for garden plants. Today, however, this is true only in regions with clean air. In many countries the atmosphere is polluted by industrial waste products. Among the most dangerous of these products is an oxide of sulphur which, in combination with water, produces the acid rain that is highly injurious to most plants. Rainwater also contains other toxic substances which invade it through absorption of dust particles in the air or the flushing of dust waste from roofs. If such water is used for watering, it gradually makes the soil more acid, so greater attention needs to be given to liming the soil, especially if you are growing plants that need neutral or alkaline soil. Rainwater that runs off farming land that has been treated with powerful herbicides is also unsuitable for plants. Even the relatively pure and safe water from your domestic water supply or from a deep well is potentially harmful if it is too cold. If used directly, it cools the soil too much and slows the biological activity of your plants. Ideally, this water should first be stored in a tank so that it can warm to a suitable temperature.

In view of the individual water requirements of different species of plants, it will often be better to water particular parts of a bed or border with a watering-can rather than to drench the whole area with a hose. In this way each plant or group of plants

◀ The Aquaprogramme irrigating set with various spraying attachments.

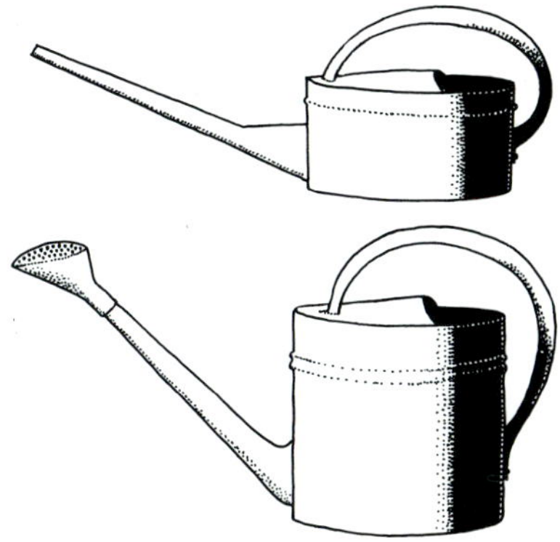

A greenhouse watering-can and garden watering-can.

can be watered according to its particular need. Hose-fed sprinklers are, however, a great help when you need to water bigger areas of plants with similar water needs, especially during long dry periods. In general it is best to use a sprinkler that produces a fine spray so that the drops of water are small enough to warm up in the air before falling onto the plants.

The best time to water is late afternoon, so that the plants can make the good use of water from the soil overnight. If you have to water your plants directly from the water tap, whether by can, hose or sprinkler, do it early in the morning, particularly in hot summer weather. At that time the plants and soil are still relatively cold after the night, so they will not suffer the thermal shock they would undergo if watered in the afternoon heat.

A quick watering, no matter how frequent, is in general much less beneficial than a thorough, if less frequent, drenching, which enables the moisture to get to the roots of the plants. Avoid sprinkling water directly on to the flowerheads of plants.

For plants such as chrysanthemums whose leaves, when sprayed with water, are vulnerable to the development of fungal diseases, it is best to use a can without a sprinkler head, directing the water around the base of the plants.

Circular garden irrigator and portable drum for storing a hose.

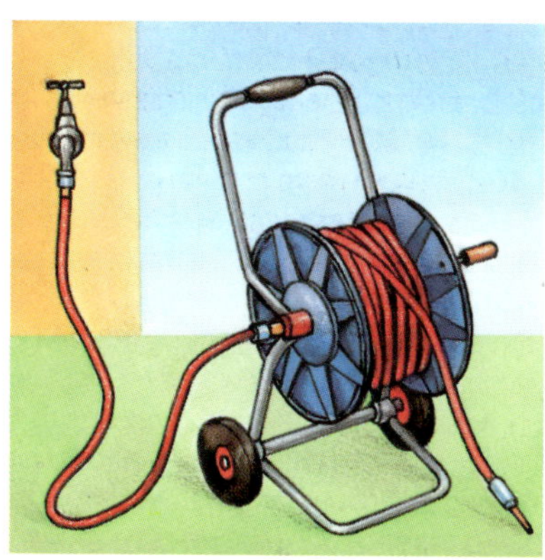

6 Basic Plant Needs: Nutrients

Plants require a number of nutrients in order to grow and reproduce. The most important are carbon, oxygen and hydrogen, acquired from the air and from water, and nitrogen, phosphorus, potassium, calcium, magnesium, sulphur and iron, which are drawn with water from the soil. Plants use these nutrients to create sugars (carbohydrates) and other organic compounds. Other nutrients, the so-called trace elements, such as manganese, boron, copper, zinc and molybdenum, are also needed, but in much smaller amounts.

Nutrients are essential for a variety of physiological functions. For instance, nitrogen stimulates growth of stems and leaves; phosphorus the general growth process, including root development and the ripening of flowers and seeds; potassium the process of photosynthesis whereby a plant manufactures carbohydrates in its leaves; potassium also contributes vitally to the quality of a plant's flowers and fruits and its resistance to disease. Lack of, or even an excess of, nutrients has a negative effect on growth, flowering and the health of flowers. A balanced diet of nutrients is therefore a basic precondition of successful growing.

Achieving this balance depends on the presence of sufficient nutrients in the soil and on the ability of plants to absorb and process them in the required proportions. The supply of nutrients naturally occurring in the soil is unlikely to be enough to feed an intensively stocked bed or border of flowering plants. That is why the soil needs to be given regular supplies of fertilizers, together with garden compost or well-rotted manure to maintain the soil structure. There is a wide variety of proprietary brands of fertilizers and plant feeds available from garden centres. Nitrogen is available in the form of inorganic preparations made from ammonium sulphate (which also provides sulphur), ammonium nitrate, and sodium nitrate. It is also available in organic preparations such as dried blood, hoof and horn meal, bone meal, and fish meal. Phosphorus is available as superphosphate, which also contains calcium and sulphur; it is also present in bone meal and fish meal. Potassium is available in sulphate of potash and potassium chloride; an organic source is powdered seaweed, a good soil conditioner, which also contains small quantities of nitrogen and phosphorus. Other nutrients and the trace elements are available in commercial preparations. Always use such products strictly according to the manufacturers' instructions. Always err on the side of deficiency: it is a waste of money and may be harmful to your plants to overfeed them.

You can also make your own general fertilizer that is suitable for every type of flowering plant. The recipe is: 6 parts (by weight) of superphosphate, 5 parts of ammonium sulphate, 2 parts of potassium sulphate, 1 part of magnesium sulphate, and 1 part of finely powdered bone meal. Make sure to mix these ingredients thoroughly together. Use the mixture at a rate of about 50—100 g per square metre (2—4 oz per square yard) on both seed beds and on borders you have prepared for planting out or for bedding plants. Dry fertilizers such as this should if possible be applied to moist soil and then watered in. Avoid sprinkling dry fertilizers on leaves and soft stems.

Seedlings with well-developed roots grow quicker and produce better foliage and flowers than those with weak roots.

After manuring, work a good compound fertilizer into the soil.

7 How to Make Your Own Compost

Garden compost is produced by the action of bacteria on plant and animal waste. Good compost increases the content of humus, nutrients and useful micro-organisms in the soil and improves its structure. An enormous variety of waste products is suitable as raw materials, including soft plant stems and leaves, soft prunings, cut grass, hay, straw, kitchen waste, crushed egg-shells, sawdust, wood-ash and other organic waste. Do not use flowering or seeding weeds, perennial weed roots, diseased plants, woody prunings or man-made materials such as textiles, plastics or metals. The quality of the compost will be improved if you add

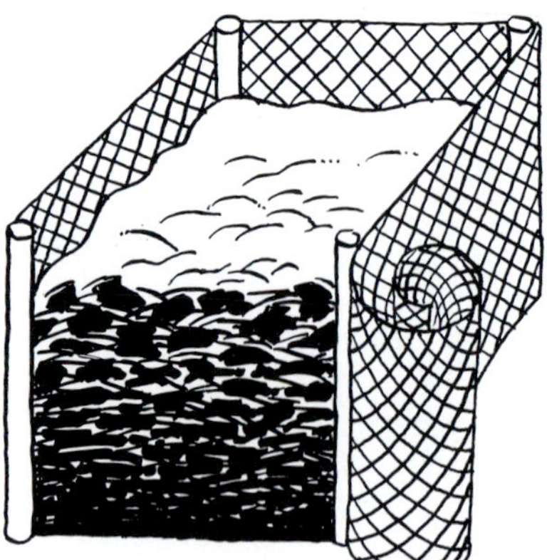

◀ Flowering plants do best in humus-rich soil.

a mixture of cattle dung, horn or bone meal, and finely crushed pine bark. Further improvement can be made by adding superphosphate and potassium sulphate fertilizers, each at the rate of 3 kg per cubic metre (6 lb per cubic yard) of compost.

A compost heap is normally started in summer for use in early winter. It is best to make a simple container consisting of wire netting arranged around four corner posts to form a cube shape 1.2—1.5 m (4—5 ft) in each dimension. Build the heap up in layers 15—30 cm (6—12 in) deep, watering each layer thoroughly and treating it with either a proprietary brand of activator or with ammonium sulphate at the rate of 15 g ($^1/_2$ oz) per layer to accelerate the process of decomposition. Finally, when the heap has reached the top of the container, cover the surface with about 5 cm (2 in) of weed-free garden soil.

The heap will have turned into compost in about 12 weeks — longer in cold weather. When ready for use it is a dark, crumbly, sweet-smelling material of consistent structure. In the process of decomposing, compost requires 40—60 per cent moisture. If it seems to be getting too dry, particularly in extended periods of dry weather, carefully moisten the heap with water or, better still, with a solution of nitrogen fertilizer, liquid manure or poultry-dung fodder. Keep the compost heap free of weeds at all times.

The principal use for this compost will be for improving and enriching the soil in beds and borders during the growing season in spring and summer. But in winter it can also be used as a mulch to keep the soil warm and prevent it from drying out.

Pile composting materials into an area fenced off with galvanized wire-meshing, halved sticks or corrugated plastic boards.

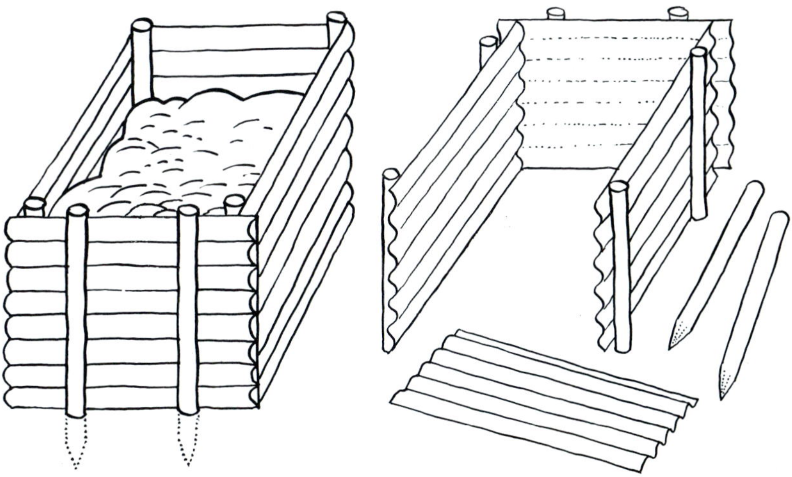

8 The Gardener's Enemies: Plant Pests and Diseases, and Weeds

Today the trend is firmly in the direction of ecologically sound ways of dealing with plant diseases and pests; that is, to use treatments and methods that have little or no side effects that could damage other plants or animals. The first rule is that prevention is better than cure: if you use healthy seeds and plant healthy seedlings, bulbs and tubers, you are much less likely to have trouble later on. It is good practice to steam the soil used for pre-cultivated seedlings at a temperature of 90—100°C two to three weeks before sowing. Treat bulbs, corms and tubers for three hours in a pink solution of hypermangan or for 15 minutes in a suitable disinfectant such as benomyl.

Important preventive measures include sowing and planting at the right time and at the correct distance apart. Flowers that are prone to diseases transmitted through the soil, such as dianthus and sweet peas are to fusarium wilt, should be grown in a different bed or border every year, returning to the original site only at five-year intervals.

Leaves of plants stricken with fungal diseases should be removed and burnt immediately. Plants stricken with viral diseases, which show as deformations or coloured spots on the leaves or flowers, must be removed in their entirety (including roots) and burnt because they cannot be treated. Remove and destroy beetle larvae and caterpillars. Slugs can be caught in specially made traps; or you can make your own with cups filled with beer and embedded in the soil. Avoid using slug poisons: they will also poison thrushes and other birds that eat slugs and snails; and they harm hedgehogs, which also prey on slugs.

In general, pesticides and other chemical poisons should be used very sparingly — and then only if the diseases or pests exceed a tolerable limit and mechanical or biological methods of protection no longer suffice. The most suitable chemical preparations are those that are least poisonous and harmful to man and other animals. They should, for instance, be as highly selective as possible, if possible acting only against the specific disease or pest that is causing the trouble.

Follow the manufacturer's instructions exactly when using pesticides. A liquid spray must be used in the correct concentration, at the most appropriate time and in dry and preferably windless weather. When working with these substances, observe the basic hygiene rules and use rubber gloves, face masks and other recommended protective aids. Weedkillers (herbicides) should not be used because they are a risk and may also damage desirable plants and poison the soil. The most appropriate method is mechanical removal of weeds when working the soil in the autumn and removing them with a hoe during the growing season.

◀ These yellow streaks on the red flowers are symptoms typical of several viral diseases of tulips as well as of other bulbous plants.

Place boxes in the garden for songbirds in winter and give them appropriate other seeds in the feed-troughs.

Various types of sprays for protecting plants against diseases and pests.

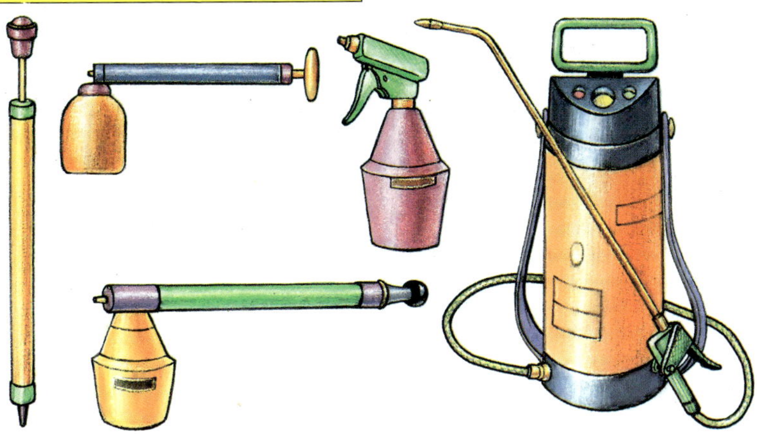

A typical small greenhouse.

9 Gardening under Glass

A greenhouse and/or a cold frame greatly extend the scope of the amateur gardener. All the most popular pot plants can be grown in a greenhouse given minimum temperatures between frost-free and about 7°C. These include a host of tender bulbous plants and annuals as well as tender greenhouse shrubs and perennials, even including some orchids. The greenhouse is also invaluable for plant propagation of every kind, for producing bedding plants, and for storing plants during the winter. Specially heated greenhouses further extend the range of plants that you can grow.

Most domestic greenhouses today are constructed from prefabricated components made of aluminium alloy or cedarwood frames, with glass ready-cut to size, and are quite easy to assemble. Light-weight or portable greenhouses, and also cold frames, are often glazed with clear plastic, which is cheaper and less fragile than glass. Glass, however, traps the sun's warmth more efficiently than plastic and also retains artificially created heat better. For a typical domestic greenhouse about 3 x 2.4 m (10 x 8 ft) in ground area a glass-to-ground structure is cheaper and more versatile than one with a base wall of brick or timber boarding — though the latter may be more economical for a heated greenhouse in a cold area. The greenhouse may rest on a concrete or brick floor covering the whole internal area; alternatively, you may wish to use the soil for raising plants, in which case you may choose to have a concrete or gravel path down the centre of the greenhouse. If the floor is paved throughout, you can fit staging (working surfaces) along the longest sides.

This, too, is readily available from greenhouse manufacturers. The commonest design of greenhouse is of a rectangular shape with a pitched roof and vertical sides. Free-standing greenhouses should be sited in an open, sunny position, with the longer axis running east-west; this allows it to exploit winter sunlight most effectively. Lean-to greenhouses should be sited against south-facing house or garden walls. Good ventilation is vital in a greenhouse. The typical domestic structure should have at least two adjustable vents — one in a side wall and one in the roof. You will also need a maximum-and-minimum thermometer, which allows you to keep an eye on fluctuations of temperature within the greenhouse.

Unheated greenhouses allow you to grow a very wide range of hardy and half-hardy plants, but favourites such as carnations, chrysanthemums, and even some alpines need artificial heat. A wide range of heating systems is available. Electric heaters are most convenient, but gas heaters are also widely used. Lean-tos attached to a house wall can, of course, be fitted with an extension to the house central-heating system. Whatever your artificial heat source, it is essential that the system has thermostatic controls to enable you to provide optimum temperatures for the particular plants you are growing. You can conserve heat in winter, and thus reduce your heating bills, by lining the interior of the greenhouse with thin, transparent PVC or polythene sheets. Try to ensure that there is a gap of 12—25 mm ($^1/_2$—1 in) between the plastic and the glass and that the air in the gap is sealed in. The aim is to achieve the effect of double glazing, the air layer providing heat insulation. Remove this lining when the weather warms up in late spring.

A garden frame needs only two or three windows in its sloping, hinged lid. It should be situated on a sunny site protected from the wind, with windows facing south. A complete frame can be purchased, or the hinged, glazed lid and walls can be made from timber (preferably hardwood). The windows may be of glass or transparent plastic. The simplest frame relies on sunlight to heat it. But you can buy inexpensive electric soil-warming cables to provide frost-free conditions throughout the winter, enabling you to grow plants out of season or to start your spring-flowering plants earlier. In spring, use the unheated frame for your pots and trays of half-hardy seedlings that need protection while hardening off. In summer a shaded frame is ideal for raising cuttings.

Collect rainwater from the roof of the greenhouse via guttering and downpipe into a water butt. Make a gravel soakaway under the water butt to drain any overflow.

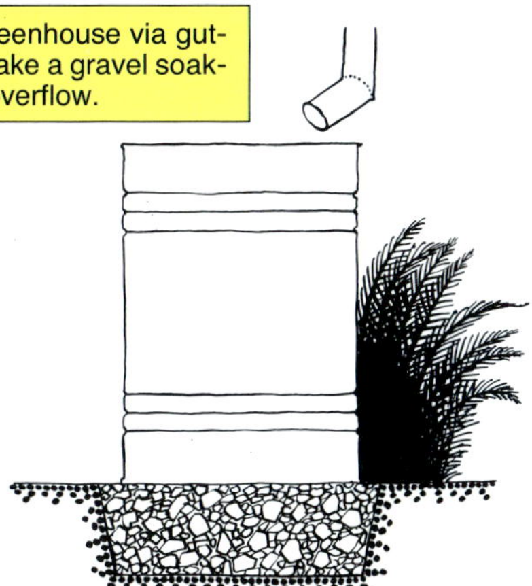

A simple frame for growing and hardening off seedlings and young plants.

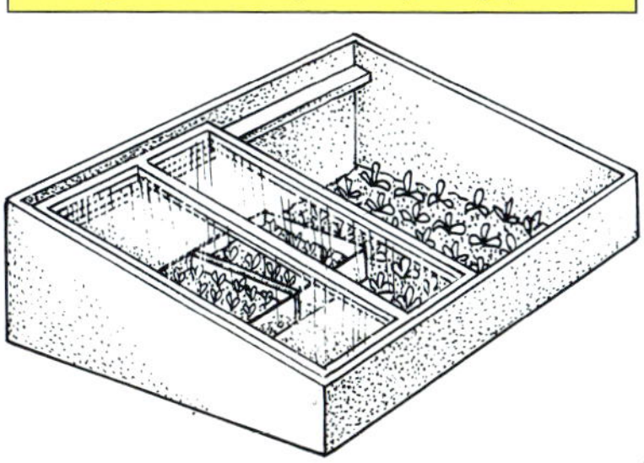

10 Perennials: Their Place in the Garden

Perennials play an essential role in every garden, large or small. Tended properly, most will last for five years or more. Perennials are valuable not only for their flowers but also, in many cases, for their attractive foliage and habit of growth. Moreover, among the thousands of widely different species and varieties available, you can select a range of plants that will give you flowers from spring right through to the winter.

In a more or less formal design of garden, perennials are usually planted in regularly shaped beds bordering a lawn, paths or hedges, or against the walls of buildings. In those beds and borders accessible only from one side it is obviously sensible to locate low-growing plants at the front and taller plants at the back. Today, however, the trend in garden design is away from too rigid a formality towards the more informal effect of the so-called 'cottage garden' where colours, shapes and sizes are mixed in a much freer arrangement. Such designs may include herbaceous borders, which consist mainly of perennials, and mixed borders, which are mainly a combination of perennials and shrubs. Taller perennials of an 'architectural' character, decorative grasses, the taller bulbous and tuberous plants and various long-flowering annuals may be situated in a bed which is no more than 1.5 m (5 ft) deep. The annuals should be planted after the bulbs in order to fill any empty places left on the bed after the long-term residents have been sited. Neighbouring clumps of perennials should be mixed in such a way that the colours of their flowers harmonize.

Small, narrow beds can be used for planting one species of perennial in one or several varieties, or a small number of species that combine pleasingly in terms of shape and colour. Attractive backgrounds for regular perennial beds include single-coloured walls, coniferous trees with branches reaching the ground, freely growing decorative bushes or clipped hedges, and painted ornamental fencing and trellises.

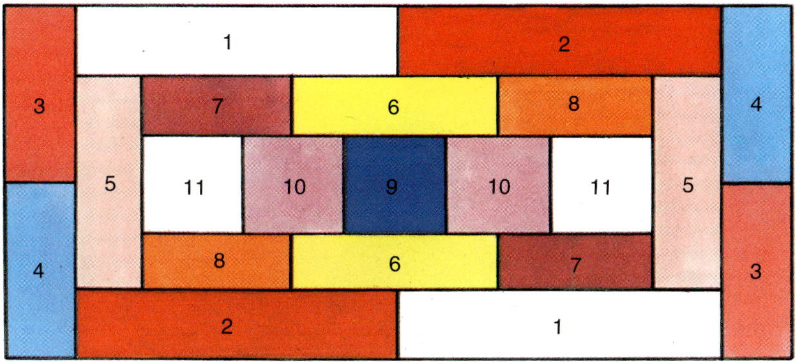

A bed of formally planted perennials: (1, 2) pink (*Dianthus plumarius*); (3, 4) aster (*Aster*); (5) bergenia (*Bergenia cordifolia*); (6) leopard's bane (*Doronicum columnae*); (7) pyrethrum (*Pyrethrum roseum,* syn. *Chrysanthemum coccineum*); (8) geum (*Geum*); (9) iris (*Iris*); (10) blazing star (*Liatris spicata*); (11) Shasta daisy (*Chrysanthemum maximum*).

An informally planted bed of perennials: (1) leopard's bane (*Doronicum columnae*); (2) lupin (*Lupinus* x *hybridus*); (3) aster (*Aster yunnanensis*); (4) Shasta daisy (*Chrysanthemum maximum*); (5) phlox (*Phlox paniculata*); (6) coral flower (*Heuchera sanguinea*); (7) *Coreopsis verticillata;* (8) bishop's wort (*Stachys macrantha*); (9) *Aubrieta deltoidea* hybrids; (10) stonecrop (*Sedum telephium*).

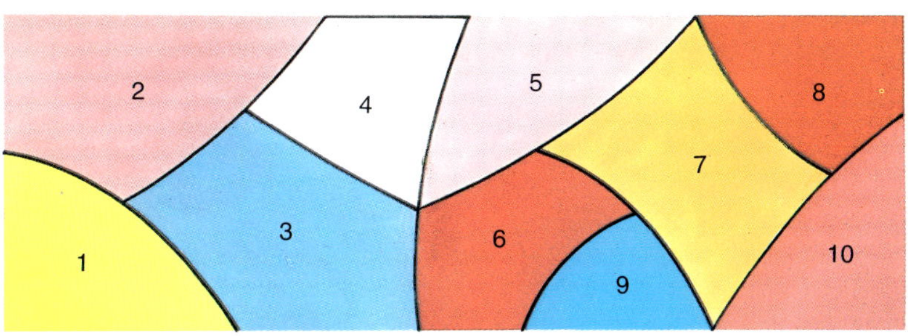

11 Perennials: Planning and Siting

It is usually best to grow perennials in free clumps on irregularly shaped beds around country cottages or in freely arranged modern gardens. But be careful to consider the configuration of the terrain. For example, free-shaped clumps of flowers can be located on higher sites to create a transition between grasses and woody plants. The normal procedure is to create a 'carpet' foundation of irregularly shaped spaces of various sizes with prostrate and other low-growing perennials, especially those with lovely foliage. Then, among these, you can plant individual or clumps of taller plant species so as to achieve a harmonious whole of both shape and colour. Choose the various species carefully to produce a pleasingly colourful effect throughout the year.

●

Colour diagrams are a useful aid in planning to create colour harmony amongst perennials, bulbs, annuals and shrubs in your beds and borders. For example, if your 'starting' colour is yellow, a suitable complementary colour is violet. Both colours are also compatible with the adjacent complementary colours shown in the diagram (blue and red). White is suitable as a transition between colours (such as blue and

◀ *Delphinium* varieties often look best if grown in solitary groups.

A diagram to aid selection of flower colours.

violet) which do not harmonize. Light yellow and light orange blend with all other colours. As a general principle, it is best to place light colours at the front of a bed and dark ones at the back.

Taller perennials and those with especially conspicuous flowers can be planted individually or in smaller clumps in places where they can act as a dominant feature and attract attention. For example, they can be sited in a bed at the end of a straight path, by the side of garden steps or seat, in a small 'cut-out' in a lawn, or as the centrepiece of a bed of cushion-like perennials or low-growing bulbous flowers. They can also be planted among free clumps of shorter perennials, or as individual specimens in paved areas. Examples of good 'feature' perennials of this kind include the foxtail lily (*Eremurus*), various *Delphinium* hybrids, *Yucca, Helenium,* the taller Michaelmas daisies (*Aster novae-angliae*), goat's beard (*Aruncus*), and some euphorbias, hellebores and verbascums. Of the lower plants, suitable choices include dittany or burning bush (*Dictamnus*), oriental poppy (*Papaver orientale*) and some short grasses such as porcupine grass (*Miscanthus sinensis*).

An informally disposed group of perennials on a lawn: (1) *Delphinium* Elatum variety; (2) *Delphinium* Belladonna variety; (3) primrose (*Primula vulgaris*); (4) pyrethrum (*Chrysanthemum coccineum*); (5) *Coreopsis grandiflora;* (6) Michaelmas daisy (*Aster novi-belgii*); (7) *Aubrieta deltoidea* hybrid; (8) fleabane (*Erigeron speciosus*); (9) peony (*Paeonia lactiflora* variety); (10) Chrysanthemum (*C. indicum*) variety; (11) phlox (*Phlox paniculata*); (12) gold dust (*Alyssum saxatile*); (13) moss phlox (*Phlox subulata*); (14) iris (*Iris*); (15) Chinese juniper (*Juniperus chinensis* 'Old Gold').

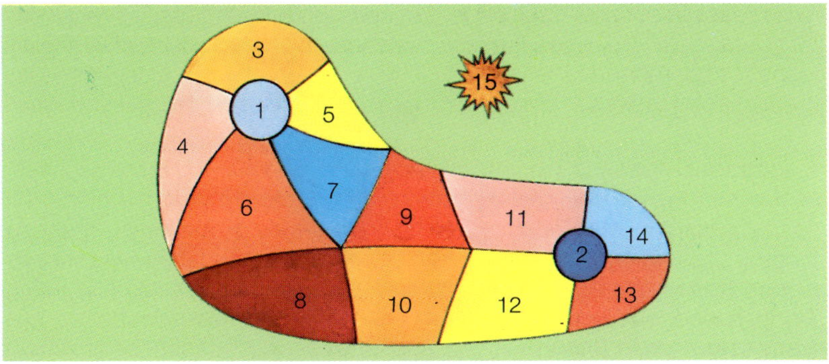

12 Perennials: Planting and Maintenance

In view of the fact that perennials remain in situ for 4—5 years or even longer, you need to prepare the soil before they are planted. Dig the soil to a depth of 25—30 cm (10—12 in), picking out the stems and roots of perennial weeds. If necessary, improve the soil composition (see hint no. 2), digging in 3—5 kg (6—11 lb) of garden compost and 30—50 g (1—1 $^{3}/_{4}$ oz) of compound inorganic fertilizer such as Growmore. Dig sufficiently large holes for large solitary perennials (the worse the soil, the bigger the hole) and improve the soil in them if need be.

●

Perennials flowering in spring should normally be planted at the beginning of autumn; those flowering in summer and autumn should be planted in spring. Complete your spring planting by mid-May at the latest, and your autumn planting by the end of September (or a month later in warmer regions). Protect plants against frost with a cover during autumn planting. Plants raised initially in pots can be planted out a few weeks before they come into flower. Spring-planted favourites include Japanese anemone

◀ Perennials on the edge of a pool.

(*Anemone* x *hybrida*), Michaelmas daisy (*Aster* spp.), florists' chrysanthemums (*Chrysanthemum indicum* hybrids) and varieties of Shasta daisy (*C. maximum*), lupins (*Lupinus*), pincushion flower (*Scabiosa*), golden marguerite (*Anthemis*) and catmint (varieties of *Nepeta* x *faassenii*).

In any given plot you will, of course, plant species with roughly the same demands on sun, soil, moisture, shelter and so on. Often you can mix related species to produce a riot of colour at a particular time of year. But do not forget that the planting of each bed or border needs to be planned in time as well as space. In other words, choose plants not only for colour, shape, texture, etc., but also for different flowering seasons. In this way, each plot of soil will give you colour and interest from early spring to late autumn. Plant small perennials 20—30 cm (8—12 in) apart, medium-sized ones 50—60 cm (18—24 in) apart, and the largest 80—120 cm (32—48 in) apart. When planting make an adequately large hole in your prepared soil and spread the roots of the seedling inside it. Cut off any damaged roots and shorten any that are much longer than the others. Then cover the roots with fine fertile earth to which you can add a handful of damp peat to help the plants take root. In hot, sunny weather some seedlings will need to be shaded. Water the plants in.

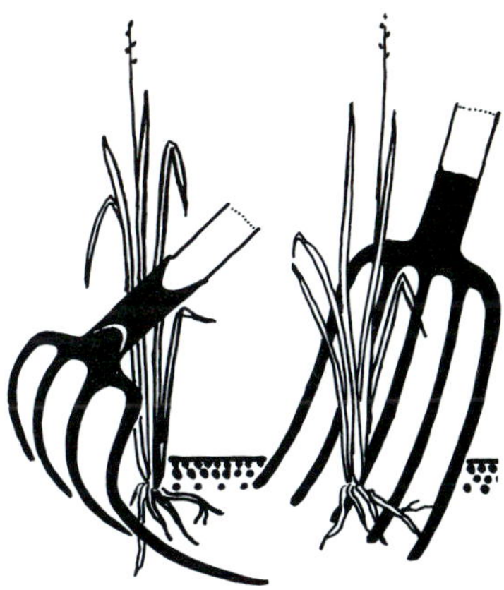

A hoe or hoeing fork is the most suitable tool for removing the underground parts of perennial weeds before planting flowering plants.

Press down soil at the roots of newly planted perennials and water the plants well.

13 Perennials: Care and Maintenance

In the first year after planting, perennials require care so that they root well, take nourishment from the soil, and produce abundant healthy flowers. During the growing season, lightly hoe and weed the soil around them. In the spring fork in compost and, if need be, add a general fertilizer at the rate of 30—40 g (1—1 $^{1}/_{2}$ oz) per square metre. Water the plants as need be, and if necessary support the taller plants with pea-sticks or bamboo poles.

●

When the flowers have faded the flower spikes should be removed from the more aggressive perennials before they set seeds; this prevents them spreading and multiplying in the plot, to the detriment of neighbouring plants. Species requiring this dead-heading include the bellflower (*Campula glomerata*), yellow loosestrife (*Lysimachia punctata*), bladder cherry (*Physalis alkekengi*), porcupine grass (*Miscanthus sacchariflorus*), and gardener's garters reed grass (*Phalaris arundinacea*). Dead-heading also encourages some species like delphiniums or *Lupinus polyphyllus* to have a second flow-

◀ If you cut off the inflorescence of the lupin immediately after it wilts, it will flower again towards the end of the summer.

ering later in the season. Cut off leafless herbaceous stems about 20 cm (8 in) above the ground and leafed ones just beneath the wilted flower. In species with woody stems, such as heather (*Calluna*), heath (*Erica*), rock rose (*Helianthemum*), candytuft (*Iberis*), lavender (*Lavandula*), lavender cotton (*Santolina*) and others, the crowns should be cut off after flowering every year to encourage the plants to grow more compact and richer flowers the following year.

●

At the end of the growing season, cut the stems of the plants right back, except for those species whose dead and faded flowers have some decorative value in winter, such as *Eryngium,* stonecrop (*Sedum telephium*) and *Senecio.* Do not cut back the stems of evergreen plants. Protect those species that are not totally frost hardy — such as red-hot poker (*Kniphofia*) and Japanese anemone (*Anemone* x *hybrida*) — by covering them with a thick layer of dried leaves, straw or bracken. Perennials liable to suffer in wet or poorly drained soil during the winter, such as foxtail lily (*Eremurus*) and *Gypsophila paniculata* and some irises, should be protected with cloches.

Restrict the spread of underground rhizomes of plants by planting them in bigger and deeper pots without a bottom or by reducing the space around them to a depth of 35—40 cm (14—16 in) with thick plastic foil.

14 Perennials: Propagation

If a perennial is to preserve its characteristic shape, size and flower colour, it must be propagated by the vegetative method. (There are some exceptions: delphiniums and lupins, for instance, can be propagated from seed.) The easiest way is division of the crowns — the part of herbaceous perennials immediately below the stems and above

Propagation of perennials by the division of crowns.

◀ Panicled phlox can be propagated from young shoot cuttings in the spring.

the roots. Crowns vary. Perennials with fibrous roots and fairly loose crowns, such as chrysanthemums, should be divided soon after flowering is finished. (If the plant flowers until late in the autumn, division should be delayed until spring.) Perennials with fleshy crowns, such as hostas and *Astilbe*, should be divided when the buds begin to shoot at the end of the dormant period.

The method is as follows. Lift out the plant with a fork, shake off as much soil as possible, and wash or hose the crown and roots clean. Now divide the crown by hand or with a knife so that each piece has enough roots and at least one or two good buds. The central, hard parts of fibrous crowns do not produce buds so should be discarded. The cut surfaces of fleshy crowns should be dusted with fungicide powder. Shorten roots that are too long or damaged. Plant out the divisions in good soil, either in the ground or in pots, as soon as possible and give them a thorough watering, before transferring them later to a permanent site.

Many perennials can be reproduced from a herbaceous cutting — that is, usually, a section of stem or a leaf bud. Only species whose young stems easily root are suitable for this purpose. Cuttings of summer- and autumn-flowering perennials should be taken in spring; those of plants that bud in spring and sprout young shoots after flowering, such as saxifrages, alyssums, aubrietas and pinks (*Dianthus*), are taken in summer.

In more rampant perennials, take a softwood stem cutting 5—8 cm (2—3 in) in length about 3 mm ($^1/_8$ in) below a bud or leaf node. Remove the lower leaves, leaving three or four at the top of the cutting. In smaller perennials make cuttings 3—4 cm (1 $^1/_4$—1 $^1/_2$ in) long, removing only the lowest leaf. Plant the bigger cuttings 3 to 4 cm (1 $^1/_4$—1 $^1/_2$ in) deep (smaller ones at a shallower depth) in boxes or pots with a proprietary seed compost or into a mixture of equal parts of peat and sand, with the surface covered with a thin layer of sand. Most herbaceous cuttings need a temperature of 13—18°C (55—64°F). Cuttings taken in summer should therefore thrive in a cold frame, but spring cuttings may need to be kept indoors or in a heated greenhouse. The cuttings should form roots in four to six weeks, but in some species root-formation may need to be encouraged by dipping the lower ends in hormone rooting powder.

Method for perennial cuttings: prepare the cutting; dip the bottom end into hormone rooting powder; plant in pots; water thoroughly.

15 Perennials: Growing from Seed

While most herbaceous perennials, especially hybrids and selected strains, are propagated from cuttings, quite a few garden favourites are grown from seed, notably bellflower (*Campanula*), columbine (*Aquilegia*), lupin (*Lupinus*), poppy (*Papaver*), and *Pulsatilla.*

Perennials whose seeds germinate slowly or whose seedlings develop slowly should be sown in February and March in bowls, trays or pots filled with proprietary seed compost. Cover the seeds with a thin layer of grit or sieved compost. Small seeds or those which require light for germination should not be covered but firmed gently into the compost with a presser board. The seeds should then be watered carefully and placed in a greenhouse, a semi-heated frame or in a room with a temperature of 10—12°C (50—54°F). At intervals, water the emerging seedlings with dilute fungicide. When the seedlings have developed one or two true leaves, prick them off into boxes or pots.

The larger seeds should normally be sown in March or April in a semi-heated frame. Those perennials whose seeds germinate quickly and whose seedlings grow quickly or do not like to be transplanted — for instance, tuberous species or those with a taproot — should be sown in April and May either in an outside seed bed, from

◀ When grown from seed, cultivars of the oriental poppy (*Papaver orientale*) rarely retain the flower colour of their parent plants, so it is better to propagate them from root cuttings.

where they can be transferred to a permanent site in spring of the following year, or sown directly into their permanent site with well-prepared soil. Plants which hate transplantation can also be sown as seedlings into pots.

Seeds which quickly loose their capacity to germinate, such as *Adonis,* bleeding heart (*Dicentra spectabilis*), hellebore (*Helleborus*) and *Pulsatilla,* should be sown immediately after ripening. Some perennials, such as globeflower (*Trollius*), trumpet gentian (*Gentiana acaulis*), aconite (*Eranthis*), lupins and certain species of lily, need their seed covers to be cracked open by frost before they can germinate. In such cases, store the seeded pots for two or three weeks outdoors before transfer to a warm room. The outer coating of the seeds of peonies, phlox, some lilies, and others must be stratified otherwise they will not sprout until the following year; sometimes the roots will develop in the first year and the stems the following spring. Mix the seeds with slightly moist sand, place them in a pot and store in a room at a temperature of about 5°C (41°F). During stratification the sand and seeds must not be allowed to dry out or freeze. In the spring, as soon as the seeds begin to germinate, sow them into adequately moist soil.

Sow fine seeds into bowls or trays. Prick off the seedlings into paper pots or cups. Sow large seeds directly into the latter.

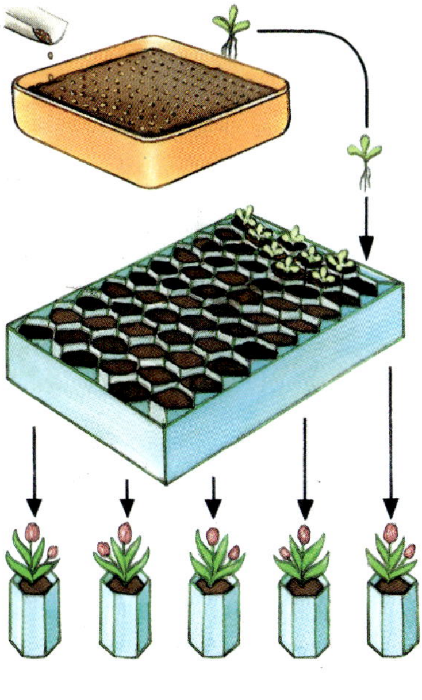

Clip off the leading shoots of seedlings grown from seeds to encourage bushy growth.

16 Perennials: Common Diseases and Pests

A white powdery fungal coating on leaves and young shoots of autumn-flowering asters, summer phlox, chrysanthemums, delphiniums, and many others, is a sign of mildew. The disease is encouraged by sudden changes in temperature, an over-dry soil, seeds sown too densely together, and over-manuring by nitrogen. Spray at once with benomyl or triforine. At the end of the season cut down and burn all diseased stems, leaves, etc., to kill off remaining traces of the fungi.

Reddish-brown spots on leaves are usually caused by one of the many *Septoria* fungi. The spots progressively get bigger, and the leaves dry out and eventually drop off. Remove the stricken leaves as early as possible and burn them; spray the plants with bordeaux mixture or any one of various suitable fungicides, and repeat the dose a couple of weeks later. Dark spots on leaves and tumours on the root-necks of stems may be of bacterial origin in plants such as phlox and peonies. Remove and burn the stricken plants. Tumours may also occur on the roots of plants of the Cruciferae family, such as gold dust (*Alyssum saxatile*), *Arabis,* and candytuft (*Iberis*) — a disease more commonly found in vegetables of the same family. Remove the plants together with the soil around the roots, treat the spot with baked lime powder and do not grow plants of this family on the site for at least five years.

Peony wilt (*Botrytis paeoniae*) turns the sprouting shoots and buds of peonies brown and makes them wither. Remove the stricken shoots well below ground level and burn them, dusting the plants' healthy crowns with bordeaux powder and spray

Mildew (*Erysiphe communis*) on the leaves of the lupin.

them with benomyl. *Botrytis cinerea, or* grey mould, attacks many other species, notably perennial euphorbias, covering infected parts with a grey velvety growth. Cut out and burn the infected shoots.

The yellowish green mosaic-like spots, mottling or ring and line patterns on the leaves of various species of perennials, such as irises, lupins, peonies, delphiniums and aquilegias, may be the result of viral diseases that are transmitted by sucking insects, such as aphids and thrips. All infected plants must be destroyed and the insect carriers controlled with the appropriate pesticides.

Aphids, thrips and various species of mites and bugs all cause deformation, distortion and other physical damage to the leaves and flowers of many perennials, as well as transmitting diseases. Greenfly-infested stems and leaves can often be cleaned with the fingers or cut off. Serious infestations should be dealt with by an appropriate pesticide that will not kill harmless insects, including those that prey on the pests. Among the most important of these is the ladybird, which preys on aphids. Often, serious infestations of aphids lead to a rapid growth in the local ladybird population.

Wireworms, which are the tiny larvae of click-beetles, inhabit mainly newly cultivated land. They live in the soil, attacking the roots of many plants, including chrysanthemums, causing yellowish brown spots to appear on the leaves, drying them up and stunting plant growth. Destroy the infested plants and protect the rest with gamma-HCH or bromophos powder insecticide.

Pick off and destroy all species of injects and their larvae. If plants are severely infested, use the appropriate insecticide.

Some common pests of perennials: (a) greenfly (*Acyrthosiphon pisum*); (b) red spider mite (*Tetranychus urticae*); (c) wireworm (*Agriotes*); (d) true bugs (*Heteroptera*); (e) thunderflies, or thrips (*Thysanoptera*); (f) cicadas (*Cicadoidea*).

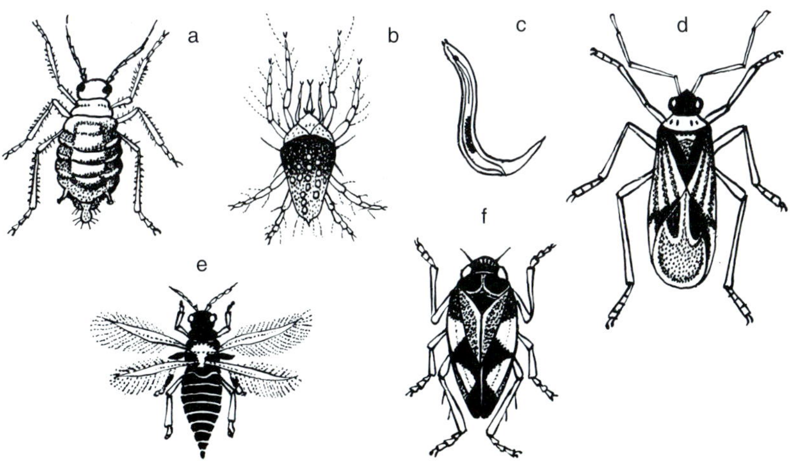

17 Perennials: Low-Growing Favourites

Low-growing perennials forming dense, attractive crowns of flowers look particularly effective alongside paths or bordering lawns. The most suitable species are those which do not spread too rampantly and have beautiful foliage as well as flowers. Examples include the yellow-flowering gold dust (*Alyssum saxatile*); the pink and white thrift called sea pink (*Armeria maritima*); the early-summer-flowering asters (purple-blue *A. alpinus* and orange-centred bright blue *A. yunnanensis*); the pink, red and white *Dianthus plumarius*; the carmine campion or German catchfly (*Lychnis viscaria*); the mauve catmint (*Nepeta* x *faassenii*); the blue alpine speedwell (*Veronica prostrata*, syn. *V. rupestris*); and the blood red coral bell (*Heuchera sanguinea*). All these have lovely flowers and most include several attractive varieties. Other favourites include the multi-coloured polyanthus hybrids of the primrose (*Primula vulgaris*); the stunted, pink *Astilbe chinensis* 'Pumila'; the lower-growing species of plantain lily (*Hosta*), such as *H. lancifolia, H. sieboldiana, H. tardiflora* and *H. undulata,* all with strikingly decorative foliage.

Attractive effects can be created in larger spaces with low, particularly trailing, perennials. Plant different species whose flowers and foliage blend well together in irregularly shaped groups. Place some paving slabs for better access to the plants.

◀ A creeping plant scheme providing an abundance of colour in spring.

Suitable trailing perennials include the many pink, red, blue and white varieties of *Aubrieta*; the white, pink and red *Arabis* x *arendsii*; the white, pink, red and violet mountain pink (*Phlox subulata*); the red rock soapwort (*Saponaria ocymoides*); the pink and white thyme (*Thymus serpyllum*); the yellow Missouri primrose (*Oenothera missouriensis*); the smaller white varieties of candytuft (*Iberis sempervirens*); lamb's tongue or woolly betony (*Stachys olympica,* syn. *S. byzantina*) with its thick greyish white hairy leaves. Plants suitable for interplanting between the above-mentioned perennials include low or medium-high grasses such as blue and saltmarsh red fescue (*Festuca*); wild oat (*Helictotrichon* sempervirens sterilis, syn. *Avena sempervirens*); feathertop or fountain grass (*Pennisetum setaceum*); and tufted hair-grass (*Eleocharis*). Good solitary plants for trailer beds are *Eremurus, Dictamnus, Verbascum, Yucca,* and *Liatris.*

Species of low perennials can also be on sites where it would be difficult to maintain a lawn. Sunny and warm sites are suitable for plants such as the snow-in-summer (*Cerastium biebersteinii*), stonecrop (*Sedum*), wild thyme (*Thymus praecox* ssp. *arcticus*), *Arabis procurrens,* mountain pink (*Phlox subulate*), speedwell (*Veronica prostrata*), cheddar pink (*Dianthus gratianopolitanus,* syn. *D. caesius*). Shaded and mainly damp soil can accommodate a lawn of periwinkles (*Vinca minor*), bugle (*Ajuga reptans*), wild ginger (*Asarum europaeum*), wood sorrel (*Oxalis acetosella*), *Waldsteinia ternata*, and others.

Primroses (*Primula*) are popular low-growing spring perennials. The Polyanthus hybrids provide brilliant shades of red, pink, blue, yellow and white.

Pink and purple moss phlox (*Phlox subulata*) and yellow gold dust (*Alyssum saxatile*) make delightful plants for the front of borders or along the edges of paths.

18 Perennials: Stocking a Cottage Garden

The authentic cottage garden may look like a glorious jumble of colourful plants, but in fact it requires careful planning in terms of plant colour, size, texture and density of planting. Typical cottage garden perennials include traditional border favourites such as the multicoloured common peony (*Paeonia officinalis*) and English primrose (*Primula vulgaris*); daisy-like yellow leopard's bane (*Doronicum plantagineum*); bleeding heart (*Dicentra spectabilis*) with its pinkish white heart-shaped flowers; the delicate white or purple spires of burning bush *(Dictamnus albus*); the multi-coloured columbines (*Aquilegia vulgaris*); the pink and scarlet painted daisy (*Pyrethrum roseum* syn. *Chrysanthemum coccineum*); the white Shasta daisy (*Chrysanthemum maximum*); blue, purple, red, pink or white larkspur (*Delphinium elatum*); variously coloured *Phlox paniculata;* tall white, pink, red or blue autumn-flowering asters (*Aster novi-belgii, A. novae-angliae*); multi-coloured small-flowered chrysanthemums (*C. corymbosum, C. rubellum*); bladder cherry or Chinese lantern (*Physalis*), decorating the garden long into the winter with orange-red lantern-like fruits. Of the annuals traditionnally found in a cottage garden, the best include snapdragons (*Antirrhinum*); China asters (*Callistephus chinensis*); *Cosmos; Zinnia angustifolia;* marigolds (*Tagetes*) and nasturtiums (*Tropaeolum majus*). Virtually all species of biennials can

◄ Bleeding heart (*Dicentra spectabilis*) is an early summer favourite in cottage gardens.

be grown in a country garden (see Hint 66). The bulbous plants to grow are daffodils (*Narcissus*), tulips, African lily (*Agapanthus* x 'Headbourne Hybrids'), orange-red crown imperial (*Fritillaria imperialis*), and lilies (*Lilium album, L. regale*). Of the small bulbs, among the best are the snowdrop (*Galanthus*), snowflake (*Leucojum*), golden garlic (*Allium moly*), grape hyacinth (*Muscari*), *Scilla* and windflower (*Anemone blanda*).

A cottage garden should reflect its recreational purpose. Much of its area may be taken up by a well-kept lawn. Around the edge of the lawn, in irregular clumps, plant flowers suitable for local conditions — for instance, the tall yellow oxlip (*Primula elatior*); white, scented lily-of-the-valley (*Convallaria majalis*); multi-coloured Russell lupins (*Lupinus*); yellow and orange varieties of globeflower (*Trollius* x *hybridus*); pink or white foxglove (*Digitalis*); yellow loosestrife (*Lysimachia vulgaris*). These will help to complement the traditional lawn-edge favourites — daffodils, snowdrops and snowflakes, grape hyacinths, pink Turk's cap lily (*Lilium martagon*). Avoid great colour contrasts; the aim is to achieve informal drifts of harmonious colours, shapes and textures.

An area of readily flowering perennials, which self-reproduce and blend well with the total garden design, makes a rewarding and easily maintained centre of interest throughout a long season, always provided you meet the environmental and cultivation needs of each of the species you select.

Shasta daisy (*Chrysanthemum maximum*).

The Maltese cross (*Lychnis chalcedonica*) is striking and attracts immediate attention with its bright colour.

19 Perennials: Late Winter and Early Spring Colour

The large-flowered Christmas rose (*Helleborus niger*) blooms from December to March, bearing saucer-shaped white flowers with yellow centres. It is 30—45 cm (12—18 in) high with seven- to nine-lobed, leathery evergreen leaves. The variety *H. niger* 'Praecox' often flowers as early as November; *H. n.* 'Potter's Wheel' from January. The Lenten rose (*H. orientalis*), slightly taller, bears flowers in colours varying from white through pink and crimson to purple in February and March. The purple hellebore (*H. purpurascens*), which blooms in March and April, has three or more drooping red and purple flowers on each stem; the green hellebore (*H. viridis*) yellow-green flowers. Hellebores do best in nutritious humus soil in a semi-shaded site where they can grow for a number of years without disturbance. Older plants respond well to composting. Hellebores are propagated by division of the crowns in March or from seeds which are sown when ripe in midsummer.

Low-growing species of primroses (*Primula vulgaris, P. juliae*) also bloom in March, with flowers on a mat of creeping ground stems. The dense, globular flower heads of the drumstick primrose (*P. denticulata*), rose-pink umbels

Bergenias are suitable for edging garden ponds.

of *P. rosea,* the yellow flowers of the oxlip (*P. elatior*) and the yellow or purple flowers of the bald primrose (*P. auricula*) bloom in March to May. Primroses grown from seed or cuttings are planted out in autumn or spring. Those propagated by division are divided after flowering and planted at once. The plants grow in any fertile soil that remains moist even in summer.

Like primroses, heartleaf bergenia (*Bergenia cordifolia*) is happiest in semi-shade, although it also does well in sunlight. It grows to a height of 30—45 cm (12—18 in) and has large heart-shaped, leathery leaves. It blooms in March and April with rich pink and purple or white flower heads. Bergenias grow in most soils, preferably not too rich. Plant between October and March in informal clumps in company with ferns, hostas, etc.

The spring-flowering blue-eyed mary (*Omphalodes verna*), yellow leopard's bane (*Doronicum plantagineum*), large-flowered barrenwort (*Epimedium grandiflorum*) with its pink, violet or yellow flowers, and Jerusalem cowslip (*Pulmonaria officinalis*) with its silver spotted leaves and blue or purple flowers, bring colour from February onwards.

Alpine and border primroses (*Primula*) offer a wide variety of flower shapes as well as colours.

20 Perennials: Late Spring and Early Summer

The shapes and colours of columbine (*Aquilegia*) flowers, particularly the garden hybrids derived from *Aquilegia vulgaris*, attract attention in the garden. They grow well in slightly damp but well-drained soil in sunlight and semi-shade. They can be propagated easily by sowing the seeds in late summer directly into the soil, or in boxes in a cold frame in March. The flowers of seeds taken from the previous year's crop do not always produce the shape and colour of the flowers of their parents. So it is sensible to grow the seedlings in a separate bed until their first flowers show and then select the best for planting into their permanent site. Vegetative propagation by division ensures the flower colours remain true to type. Plant out the divided crowns between September and March.

The pink (*Dianthus plumarius*), with its scented white, pink or red flowers, is suitable for a sunny and somewhat drier site. Clove carnations (mainly derived from *D. caryophyllus*) prefer a heavier, limy soil. Propagate by dividing the crowns in autumn.

Bleeding heart (*Dicentra spectabilis*), with its rose-red, heart-shaped flowers, looks best as a solitary plant on a lawn or among low-growing spring perennials. It should have nutritious peat-enriched soil in a semi-shaded site sheltered from strong

◀ A dense cluster of coral flowers (*Heuchera sanguinea*), with their panicles of tiny, bell-shaped flowers, has a softening effect in borders; they also make delightful bouquets. To ensure coral flowers continue to produce rich flowers, transplant them to another site after 3—5 years.

winds. Propagate by dividing the crowns and plant between October and March.

Burning bush or dittany (*Dictamnus albus*) is up to 60 cm (24 in) high with long spikes of white or purple flowers. It does well on a sunny or semi-shaded site in rich, limy soil. In warm, sunny weather the older flower heads, which are rich in oil, give off a strong lemon scent. The plant looks lovely when grown as a solitary specimen.

Lupin hybrids (*Lupinus* x *hybridus*) grow best on a sunny, protected site in nutritious, moist, lime-free soil. They bear large racemes of single or two-coloured flowers in various shades. If the wilted inflorescences are clipped off promptly, the plants flower again at the end of summer.

The modern cultivars of the oriental poppy (*Papaver orientale*) have large simple or full flowers, ranging in colour from carmine pink to orange-scarlet. After flowering, the leaves die and sprout again at the beginning of autumn. The plants grow to a height of 60—90 cm (2—3 ft) and are a dominant feature in the garden. Other lovely perennials providing colour at this time of year include pink or red coral bells (*Heuchera sanguinea*), yellow or orange globeflower (*Trollius* x *hybridus*), and pink trumpet flower (*Incarvillea*).

The trumpet flower (*Incarvillea*) will not tolerate winter damp, so plant it in free-draining soil, if necessary underlain by a layer of gravel.

Columbines (*Aquilegia*) have flowers with a distinct spur. In granny's bonnet (*A. vulgaris*) it is short and bent; but in most hybrids of this species it is long and straight.

a b

21 The Way to Success with Peonies

Peony crowns often fail to flower. The usual reason for this is that they are planted too deep. The buds on the crowns must not be more than 3 cm (1 in) below the soil surface. Peonies are planted 60—80 cm (24—30 in) apart between September and March. The site must be sunny with deep, well-drained, nutritious soil. In the first winter after planting, protect them with a thick mulch. In the growing period they require sufficient moisture, but in winter they do not tolerate wet soil. They may remain on one site for 10 or more years, and they require composting and feeding in April.

Peonies are among the most beautiful yet undemanding late-spring perennials. The 40—80 cm (16—30 in) high hybrids of *Paeonia officinalis* have white, pink or crimson flowers, some of them doubles, in May and June. The more robust hybrids of the Chinese peony (*P. lactiflora,* syn. *P. albiflora*) produce large single and double flowers in white or various shades of red or pink, some with contrasting yellow stamens; many are scented. Most of them flower from late May to July. *P. tennuifolia,* with lace-like leaves divided into delicate filamentary leaflets, is a much smaller plant, often no more than 30 cm (12 in) high. Its cultivar 'Plena' has full red flowers.

The flowers of (a) Chinese and (b) Japanese peonies (*Paeonia*).

Plant peonies are among clumps of taller perennials, such as delphiniums, chrysanthemums, and lupins. They also look good if planted as solitary plants or in small groups at the edge of lawns or in front of ornamental woody plants.

Peonies make handsome cut flowers. Cut them as soon as the blooms begin to open and keep them in a dry, cool place for 24 hours before putting them in a tall vase well-filled with water.

The rich inflorescence of this peony is proof that it has been planted at the correct depth.

22 Colourful Displays of Irises

Irises are among the most beautiful spring perennials. The taller, large-flowered garden cultivars and hybrids of bearded irises are among the most popular (the term 'bearded' refers to the fleshy hairs that form on the three outer petals). The plants grow to a height of up to 1 m (3 ft) and flower in a wide range of colours in May and June, the flowers having inner erect perianths that are the same size as the outer drooping brush leaflets.

Divide the crowns after the foliage has withered, from mid-July to mid-September. Use only the youngest part of the rhizome with the new roots, cutting off the old part. To prevent diseases, leave the rhizomes for half an hour in a solution of a suitable fungicide. Plant the rhizomes 50 cm (20 in) apart in October in a frame on a sunny or slightly shaded site about 3 cm (1 in) deep; if they are planted any deeper the plants will not bloom well. Do not trim the roots before planting. Keep the soil moist for the first month after planting, but during the winter keep the frame closed and water the plants sparingly. Shorter bearded cultivars, 20—40 cm (8—16 in) tall, and the intermediate forms 40—75 cm (16—30 in) tall, are more tolerant of damp conditions; they can be planted either in late June to early July or in September, in soil enriched with well-rotted manure, compost and bone meal.

Dwarf bearded irises — mainly hybrids of *I. chamaeiris,* 15—25 cm (6—10 in) tall, and *I. pumila,* 10—15 cm (4—6 in) tall — are suitable for drier conditions, particularly in rockeries. They come into flower from mid-April to early May.

The beardless *Iris kaempferi* does well in non-alkaline, damp and humus-rich soil at the margins of a stream or pond. It is 60—90 cm (2—3 ft) high, has deep green, narrow leaves with a rib in the middle, and large red flowers in July; the numerous hardy garden varieties have a range of flower colours.

The lofty, beardless *Iris sibirica,* 60—120 cm (2—4 ft) tall, also prefers damper soil. It has narrow grass-like leaves and bears white-veined blue flowers in June. Its many hybrids are much easier to obtain than the species. Plant them after flowering, in September or October, or in April, at a depth of 3 cm (1 in) in good moist soil in full sun. If you plant them in clumps, the rhizomes should be 60 cm (24 in) apart. The globeflower (*Trollius*) makes a suitable companion for these plants.

The flowers of various species of iris: (a) *Iris* x *barbata,* (b) *I.* x *hollandica,* (c) *I. kaempferi;* (d) seedlings prepared for planting.

Protect *Iris* x *barbata* against damp during its dormant period with a cloche or similar form of shelter.

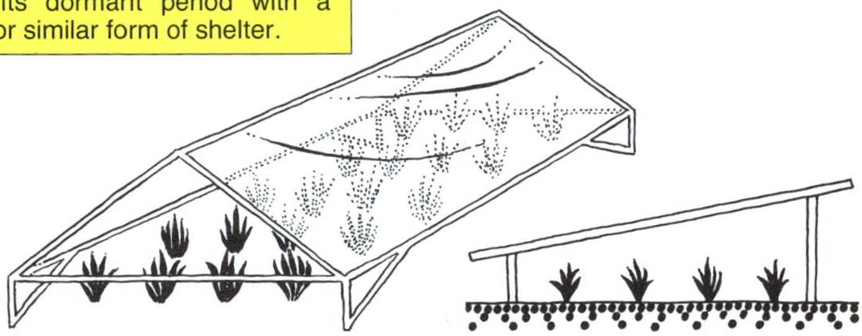

23 Perennials: Easy-to-Grow Early Summer Winners

Day lily garden hybrids (*Hemerocallis* x *hybrida*) (see picture above) are very decorative, hardy perennials 75—100 cm (2 $^1/_2$—3 ft) high. They rarely suffer from diseases or pests and even tolerate moderately poor soil. They can remain on one site, given enough space and improved soil fertility, for a number of years. The large funnel-shaped flowers, resembling lilies and mainly in various pastel colours, stay fresh only for one day, but new buds constantly appear, and the plants bloom from June to August. The plants are propagated by root division and planted between October and April. The root necks must be 2.5 cm (1 in) below the soil surface. Cut the stems down almost to ground level after the flowering period.

The cultivars of fleabane (mainly varieties of *Erigeron speciosus*), 45—60 cm (18 to 24 in) high, have flowers resembling autumn asters in various shades of blue, pink, mauve and violet, or pink and red. Removal of the dead flowers will encourage the plants to bloom again in the autumn. Propagate by dividing the crowns and plant between October and March on a sunny site with good, adequately damp, calcium-rich soil. The colourful blooms make delightful cut flowers.

Tickseed (*Coreopsis*) perennials, which are not as tall as the annual species, enliven beds with their golden yellow flowers. Threadleaf tickseed (*C. verticillata*) flowers from June to September. It is 45—60 cm (18—24 in) high; its flowers are only 4 cm (1 $^1/_2$ in) in diameter but grow in great profusion. The bright green leaves are finely divided, rather like ferns. *C. grandiflora* is 60—90 cm (2—3 ft) high and blooms from June to September. The flowers of some of its many cultivars are up to 9 cm (3 $^1/_2$ in) in diameter. This species is less tolerant of a long-term site and must therefore be transplanted more often. Tickseeds are propagated by division of the crowns in spring or early autumn. They grow best on a sunny site in fertile, well-drained soil.

The peach-leaved bellflower (*Campanula persicifolia*) grows well in a warm, semi-shaded position in good, well-drained soil. It grows to a height of 45—90 cm (18 in to 3 ft) and bears clusters of large single or double, blue or white flowers in June—July. Propagate either from cuttings of short basal shoots (essential for cultivars and double-flowered forms, which do not come true from seed), grown under glass in March—May; or from seed under glass in March to April.

Of the cornflowers (*Centaurea*), the 60—80 cm (24—32 in) high, pink-flowering *C. dealbata* and the yellow-flowered *C. macrocephala,* which is 1 m (3 ft) or more high with an inflorescence resembling a thistle, are both suitable for drier soil. The blue mountain bluet (*C. montana*) is only 30—50 cm (12—20 in) high, flowers at the end of spring and requires moister soil than the others. Cornflowers (the name is more commonly associated with annual species) are propagated by division of the crowns in spring or at the end of summer.

Maltese cross (*Lychnis chalcedonica*), which reaches a height of 90 cm (3 ft), has a burning red inflorescence from July, and makes an interesting plant for the garden. Rose campion or dusty miller (*L. coronaria*), with its carmine red or pink flowers and hairy leaves, does not last as long on one site, and requires poor, well-drained soil.

Annual and perennial cornflowers (*Centaurea*) and other perennials provide variety in growing habit, colour and period of flowering. Cornflowers shown here are perennials: (a) May- and June-flowering *C. montana,* (b) *C. dealbata,* which flowers in early summer and again in early autumn, and (c) *C. macrocephala,* with yellow blooms in early to midsummer.

24 Growing Chrysanthemums

The Shasta daisy (*Chrysanthemum maximum*) has 50—100 cm (20—40 in) high branched stems. It has elongated, sparsely toothed leaves and bears yellow-centred white flowers, 7.5 cm (3 in) or more in diameter, in the first half of July. Many garden varieties suitable for cutting are quite difficult to grow. Plant crowns from September to April; they require fertile soil on a sunny site, regular watering and a protective cover of straw or mulch in winter. They do not last long on one site, so the crowns must be divided every two or three years and transplanted in a well-prepared bed which has not been freshly manured with organic fertilizer. Proprietary fertilizers should be added during the growing season. Perennial chrysanthemums are propagated from cuttings of 5—7.5 cm (2—3 in) long basal shoots taken in March or April and raised in a peat/sand mixture in a cold frame until ready for planting out.

●

The scarlet pyrethrum (*Pyrethrum roseum,* syn. *Chrysanthemum coccineum*), unlike the Shasta daisy, grows mainly unbranched stems up to 75 cm

◀ Pyrethrum (*Pyrethrum roseum*, syn. *Chrysanthemum coccineum*).

(30 in) high. It has largely been superseded by a large number of excellent hybrids with single or double flowers in white, pink or red that are excellent for cutting. Most of the hybrids have attractive bright green, feathery foliage.

●

The flowers are occasionally attacked by mildew, which can be treated with benomyl. If the younger plants are dead-headed after flowering, they may bloom again in the autumn. Propagation is by basal shoots taken either in March or, after flowering, in July. Plant them on a sunny site with well-tilled, fertile and slightly damp soil.

●

Leopard's bane (*Doronicum plantagineum*) resembles chrysanthemums in the shape and size of its rich yellow daisy flowers, which open in April to June. It flourishes in medium-heavy, slightly damp soil on a sunny site, shaded in the summer against the mid-day heat. It is propagated by division after flowering, the crowns being planted out in September—October. Leopard's bane makes a fine show when grown with red tulips, *Brunnera macrophylla* with its blue forget-me-not flowers, primroses and other perennials that bloom at the same time. The 20—30 cm (5—12 in) high *D. columnae* flowers in April and May, and the taller great leopard's bane (*D. pardalianches*) in May and June.

The Shasta daisy (*C. maximum*) has been succeeded by its many named cultivars with single, semi-double, or double white flowers.

Leopard's bane (*Doronicum*).

25 Perennials: Mid-Summer Kaleidoscope

The many garden varieties of *Phlox paniculata* form 60—120 cm (2—4 ft) high crowns with rich panicles of white, pink, red or violet flowers of various shades, some with a different-coloured eye. They are planted in nutritious and moisture-retentive soil in a sunny position; in drier soils they fare better in semi-shaded sites. They are propagated by division of the crowns in the autumn or from herbaceous or root cuttings in spring. They sometimes suffer from mildew and leaf spot, both of which can be dealt with by proprietary treatments.

The gloriosa daisy strain of the popular black-eyed susan (*Rudbeckia hirta*) is about 60—90 cm (2—3 ft) tall and bears large yellow and reddish brown flowers, up to 18 cm (7 in) in diameter, with dark brown convex centres; it blooms from July well into autumn. Another form of gloriosa daisy has double flowers. Both forms are suitable for cutting. The coneflowers, as *Rudbeckia* are also called, flourish in well-drained soil in a sunny place. They are propagated from seeds in spring or autumn, and the seedlings planted out into their flowering site. *R. hirta* and most of its forms are short-lived, and many gardeners treat them as annuals. The gloriosa daisy form, however, will last up to three years if the crowns are covered over with sand or bracken in winter. A longer-lasting coneflower, *R. fulgida*, has several varieties producing

The coneflower (*Rudbeckia hirta* 'Gloriosa'), often listed as gloriosa daisy, flowers from midsummer to the first autumn frosts. The cut flowers also last for a long time.

mainly yellow or orange flowers with a dark centre. The related purple coneflower (*Echinacea purpurea*) bears peripheral leaflets in a purple or carmine red inflorescence about 10 cm (4 in) in diameter. The seeds are sown in March into pans and the seedlings are pricked off into boxes for hardening, then planted in a nursery bed for the summer before they are transferred to their permanent site in October. Cultivars are propagated by root cuttings taken in February, inserted in a peat/sand mixture and put in a cold frame. When young leaves appear plant them in a nursery bed before planting out in October.

The many garden varieties and hybrids of sweet bergamot, or bee balm (*Monarda didyma*), a 60—90 cm (2—3 ft) high border perennial with strongly aromatic leaves, bear dense whorls of flowers ranging in colour from violet to purple, scarlet, lavender, and pink through to white. Propagate by root division in March. Plant in moist soil in sun or part-shade. Cut down the stems after the last flowers fade in autumn.

The button snake-root, or gayfeather (*Liatris spicata,* syn. *L. callilepis*), is a highly decorative plant. About 60—90 cm (2—3 ft) high, it bears tiny pinkish purple flowers clustered densely on vertical spikes up to 30 cm (12 in) long in August and September. The plants usually come true from seeds, which are sown in a cold frame in March, hardened off, and planted out in nursery rows until ready. Alternatively, plant the crowns in a sunny position in autumn or spring, avoiding heavy soils.

Baby's breath (*Gypsophila paniculata*) is a bushy plant, 60—75 cm (2—2 $^{1}/_{2}$ ft) high, that forms a complex, open network of multi-branched stems bearing sprays of tiny flowers, double or single, pink or white according to cultivar. It requires a sunny site in well-drained, preferably alkaline soil, and looks particularly attractive when trailing over a low wall. Propagate from cuttings of 7.5 cm (3 in) long basal shoots in April or May; or from seeds.

A clump of summer-flowering perennials dominated by *Phlox paniculata.*

Blazing star (*Liatris spicata*) makes a fine show with its autumn-flowering spikes of pinkish-purple flowers.

26 Perennials: The Late Show

Typical perennials of late summer and autumn are the asters (*Aster*). The 30—45 cm (12—18 in) high Italian aster (*A. amellus*) blooms in August and September. Its many garden varieties bear flowers ranging from violet-blue to rose-pink. Much taller are the many garden varieties of Michaelmas daisy (*A. novae-angliae*), which itself may exceed 140 cm (4 $^1/_2$ ft) in height. The flowers, pink, red, bluish violet or white, bloom in September. The other Michaelmas daisy (*A. novi-belgii*), has bald herbaceous stems and somewhat smaller flowers which do not close at night. The *A. dumosus* is only 20—60 cm (8—24 in) high and, because of its compact growth and rich flowers, it is used as a border plant, for spatial planting and at the front of informal plantings and rockeries. Asters like a sunny site. *A. novi-belgii* prefers damp clayey soil, cool, damp air and an airy site, otherwise it gets mildew. All species of asters are propagated by division of the crowns in spring. They last a long time on one site.

The sneezewort (*Helenium autumnale*) forms 60—150 cm (2—5 ft) high herbaceous stems which branch out on the upper part into yellow to brownish-red flowerheads with convex, darker centres. It is nowadays represented in gardens by a wide range of colourful hybrids and varieties. All require a sunny site with fertile, adequately damp soil. Divide and plant the roots between October and April. Some of the earliest-flowering forms will bloom again later if they are cut back when the first flowers fade.

The garden forms of Japanese anemone (*Anemone* x *hybrida*) have 60 to 120 cm (2—4 ft) high herbaceous stems with many pink, white or red flowers. They are propagated by division of the crowns and are planted between October and March on a semi-shaded, protected site with moist but free-draining soil. Protect them against winter frosts. (Note that some of these forms are incorrectly listed as *A. japonica.*)

The 90—120 cm (3—4 ft) high common monkshood (*Aconitum napellus*) has racemes of mainly dark violet, hood-shaped flowers. Garden forms are more readily available than the species. The 'Bicolor' variety has blue and white flowers; some others have white ones. Monkshoods require moist, deep soil in semi-shade. They are propagated by division in autumn or spring. Monkshoods are highly poisonous in every part, so must be handled with care.

Stonecrops (*Sedum*) are suitable for planting in perennial beds and free clumps. The garden forms of *S. spectabile* are 30—45 cm (12—18 in) high and have bluish-grey fleshy leaves which turn golden yellow in the autumn. The flowers vary from pink to dark red. The somewhat similar *S. telephium,* with greyish-green leaves, has purple-red inflorescences. Both these stonecrops flower in September and October; their flowers retain much of their colour in winter so it is better not to clip the plants until spring. Propagate by division and plant the crowns in autumn or in spring; *S. telephium*, in particular, needs moist but free-draining soil.

A well-established stonecrop (*Sedum spectabile*) makes a fine showing with its large heads of small pink flowers.

Italian aster (*Aster amellus*) is a typical hardy herbaceous perennial flowering at the end of summer and the beginning of autumn.

27 Autumn-Flowering Chrysanthemums

Two of the most widely grown of the autumn-flowering perennial chrysanthemums are *C. rubellum* and the moon daisy *C. serotinum* (syn. *C. uliginosum*). Both bear comparatively small flowers — 4—5 cm (1 $^1/_2$—2 in) in diameter — which are more suitable for decorating the garden because they are more resistant to autumn and winter frosts than the large-flowered forms. Both have many cultivars. All grow best in places with a long, warm autumn. *C. rubellum* and its cultivars reach a height of 45—75 cm (1 $^1/_2$ to 2 $^1/_2$ ft) and produce mainly single, fragrant flowers varying in colour from yellow to pink, bright crimson and red-purple. The moon daisy, one of the tallest chrysanthemums, grows to a height of 185 cm (6 ft), forming clumps of erect, elegant plants with narrow, lobed leaves and bearing white, daisy-like flowers well into November.

Chrysanthemums are planted between September and April in a sunny site in good, well-drained neutral or alkaline soil. The plants are propagated in March and April by 5—7.5 cm (2—3 in) long cuttings of basal shoots inserted in a mixture of equal parts of peat and sand and placed in a cold frame;

◄ The small, daisy-like flowers of alpine and some other chrysanthemums.

they can be planted out when the cuttings are well rooted. The plants should be lifted every three years, divided and replanted.

In May or early June, when the young plants are no more than 20 cm (8 in) high, they should be 'stopped' — that is, the growing tip of each plant must be pinched out to encourage side shoots to develop. The plants will develop an even bushier habit if, a little later, the growing tip of each side shoot is stopped, triggering the growth of secondary side shoots or laterals.

Feed the young plants with general inorganic fertilizer in liquid form, using a watering can without the sprinkler head to direct the liquid at the roots. Do not over-water but ensure the soil is adequately moist. In winter protect the plants against frost with a cover of conifer branches or straw. Do not remove the cover until the beginning of April because the young shoots are sensitive to spring frosts. In spring, rake the soil around the roots, which often become partly exposed after several years of growth.

These perennials, especially their hybrids and varieties, make excellent cut flowers. For the specialist, however, the perennials described in hint no. 28 are the best for display purposes.

Various types of *Chrysanthemum* flowers, from a single form at top left to 'exhibition incurved' (bottom left) and 'thread-petalled' (bottom right).

28 Florists' Chrysanthemums

These are the chrysanthemums, often with immense, globular heads with masses of densely packed petals, that have been bred in the first instance for exhibition purposes and are often the main attraction at local flower shows. Most of these have been derived from *C. indicum*, *C. vestitum* and other oriental species.

●

These varieties are half-hardy if grown in the border, though they are hardy if raised in a greenhouse. The early-flowering varieties are grown outdoors, the late-flowering ones under glass. Florists' chrysanthemums are further subdivided into groups according to the types and sizes of blooms. The outdoor varieties can be grown in the ground, which must be dressed in spring with a base fertilizer, or in containers filled with a suitable potting compost. Plant them out in late April or early May, about 30—45 cm (12—18 in) apart, and support them with sticks or canes as they grow. The plants must be watered thoroughly every six or seven days except in periods of continuous rain, and fed with liquid organic fertilizer every 10 days or so from early June until the flower buds start to reveal their colour. Greenhouse varieties are container-grown in potting compost from March; they should be potted on into larger pots after about a month and into still larger pots in May. At the final potting, support the plants with canes. The pots can be placed outdoors from June until the end of September. As with the outdoor varieties, the plants need feeding with a compound liquid fertilizer from June to September. Take care not to over-feed. Water the plants regularly — every 48 hours, or more frequently in hot, dry weather. Do not allow florists' chrysanthemums to develop too many stems.

●

The outdoor varieties should be restricted to five or six flowering stems as soon as they can be trimmed without injuring the plant. The greenhouse varieties should be trimmed in July or the beginning of August so that each plant has only four stems. The production of the largest flowers requires 'disbudding' of each flower stem — that is, the removal of all buds and side shoots except for the central bud on each stem. Outdoor varieties are disbudded from the end of July, greenhouse varieties in September and October.

Pinching out side leaves on a chrysanthemum.

Removing the side buds on a chrysanthemum.

29 Perennials as Focal Points

Among the most beautiful perennials to use as solitary or small-group focal points in the garden are the various races of hybrids derived from crosses between *Delphinium elatum* and *D. grandiflorum.* The tallest of these races, from the large-flowered 'Elatum' group, may reach a height of 2.5 m (8 ft) with spires of flowers more than 30 cm (12 in) long. Medium tall varieties, notably the Pacific Hybrids, are 1.5—2 m (4 $^1/_2$—6 $^1/_2$ ft) tall, while the smaller varieties range from 90 cm (3 ft) to 1.5 m (4 $^1/_2$ ft). The colours of these varieties range from pure white through pink and silvery grey, to blues and purples; many have a contrasting 'eye' colour. Most flower in June and July; some, if cut back after flowering, will bloom again in August or September. Plant in September to March in good, deep soil in a sunny, preferably sheltered site. All the hybrids need staking. Propagate delphinium perennials from basal cuttings in April. The Pacific Hybrids are generally short-lived; some gardeners treat them as annuals, raising them from seed.

Adam's needle (*Yucca filamentosa*) has a big, exotic-looking inflorescence with many creamy white bell-shaped flowers at the height of summer. It forms a big crown of long, evergreen leaves. Plant it in April or October on a sunny site with free-draining and not too rich soil. Protect the roots with a cover of leaves in winter. Propagate

◀ A *Yucca* in full summer flower makes a striking focal point in the garden.

The burning bush or dittany (*Dictamnus albus*) looks best when grown as a medium high solitary plant. Its old flower heads are rich in aromatic oils which emit a strong scent on still summer evenings.

in spring by detaching well-developed rooted suckers and planting them in their permanent site.

Mullein (*Verbascum olympicum*) also looks good on sunny and warm sites. About 2—2.5 m (6—8 ft) high, it is a long-living plant with grey, felt-like foliage and tall, branching spikes of deep yellow flowers from June into September. Other fine mulleins are the hybrids derived from *V. phoeniceum*, with colours including white, gold, pink, orange, maroon and purple. Verbascums are resistant to frost but do not tolerate winter damp and sudden changes in temperature. Propagate *V. olympicum* by seeds sown in April in seed compost, gradually hardened off in the summer, and planted out in September. The hybrids must be propagated from root cuttings in February or March and then dealt with in the same way as the seeds prior to autumn planting on site.

Globe thistle (*Echinops ritro*) tolerates drought and poor soil. Its herbaceous stems with thorny, toothed grey-green leaves resemble those of the thistle. It grows to a height of 90—120 cm (3—4 ft) and in July and August it has metallic-blue globular flowers. Plant it from October to March on a free-draining sunny site in free natural clumps; it looks particularly good with yellow-flowering, dry-loving perennials such as fernleaf yarrow (*Achillea filipendulina*) and goldenrod (*Solidago*). Propagate by dividing the crowns between October and March. The orange sunflower (*Heliopsis scabra*) has coarse hairy stems and grows to a height of 90—120 cm (3—4 ft). Its many excellent varieties produce flowers ranging from lemon to orange-yellow from July to September. They grow well on a sunny or lightly shaded site with moderately damp soil. Cut down the flowering stems in November. Propagate by dividing the crowns in spring.

The large-flowered Elatum hybrids of *Delphinium* make some of the most beautiful solitary perennials.

30 Perennials for Semi-Shaded and Shaded Sites

Astilbes make delightful plants for shaded sites (though they also thrive in sun). The best to use are the varieties of the garden hybrid *A.* x *arendsii.* These grow to a height of 60—90 cm (2—3 ft) and bear loose, pyramid-shaped spires of tiny white, pink, mauve or red flowers in June to August. They need a permanently damp soil (beside a pond or stream is ideal) and frequent watering in summer. A moisture-retentive mulch applied in spring will also help. Plant between mid-autumn and early spring, and cut down the plants to ground level in October.

Goat's beard (*Aruncus dioicus*) does best in semi-shade. Its height (120—180 cm/4—6 ft) and unusual inflorescence make it useful as a solitary plant. The mature plants look highly effective when in June they form great airy, rich plumes of tiny creamy white flowers. The male plants have a richer inflorescence than the female ones. Goat's beard grows best in deep, moist soil; like the astilbes, it is happy beside a pond. Propagate by dividing the crowns at the end of summer or in spring.

◀ *Astilbe.*

The lily-of-the-valley (*Convallaria majalis*) is popular for its delicate, pleasantly scented white or pink flowers that bloom in April and May. Propagate it from underground rhizomes terminating in a shoot. Plant them 7.5—10 cm (3—4 in) apart in autumn in soil enriched with compost or leaf mould. The best site is under deciduous trees where they can spread. Lilies-of-the-valley can be speeded up in growth. In mid-autumn plant 10 cm (4 in) long rhizomes with thick three-year shoots in pots filled with equal parts of leaf mould and loam and a small quantity of sharp sand and place in the greenhouse or frame. Then in January bring the pots indoors or into a greenhouse with a temperature of about 20°C (68°F), watering the shoots to encourage rapid growth.

Bugbanes (*Cimicifuga*) grow to a height of 60—200 cm (2—6 ft), depending on the species, and develop plume-like spikes of small white, cream, or palest yellow flowers in July, August or September. They are planted in semi-shaded positions from autumn to early spring in moist, leafy soil. They can be propagated by root division.

Meadow rue (*Thalictrum aquilegiifolium*) is 60—90 cm (2—3 ft) high. In May and June it forms dense panicles, 15—20 cm (6—8 in) long, of small mauve or pink flowers. The species and its numerous varieties (which have flowers in white and various shades of purple) have attractive grey-green foliage. Propagate by dividing the crowns in March or April, and plant in rich, moist soil in light shade.

Speeding up the growth of pot-grown lily-of-the-valley (*Convallaria*).

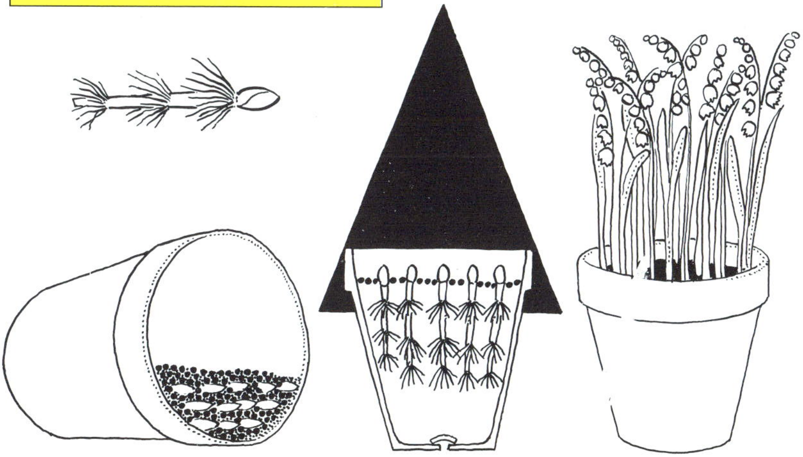

31 Using Ornamental Grasses in the Garden

Ornamental grasses have a decorative effect in the garden mainly because of their structure and leaf colours. The leaves are mostly in various shades of green, but blue, silver grey, yellowish or bronze brown grasses are also available. Some cultivars have leaves with crosswise or lengthwise stripes; others turn a vivid shade of yellow, orange or brown in the autumn. A few have attractive inflorescences.

Plant ornamental grasses in heath gardens, and even in mixed borders, where their light, airy shape will not overhelm shorter, denser plants. Tall clumps are suitable as solitary plants; or you can plant medium-high ones in free clumps. The low-growing species can look effective in rockeries. Perennial grasses are often planted with some annuals.

Propagate most perennial grasses by dividing and planting them in spring. The divided parts should not be too small. Do not shorten the roots. The plants need plenty of moisture during sunny weather while they are taking root. Plant the potted seedlings at any time during the growing season.

Grasses do not require any great care in the growing saason. Do not feed undemanding species such as wild oat (*Helictotrichon sempervirens*) and

◀ Delicate stems with small inflorescences give an airy effect in the garden.

blue or red fescue (*Festuca*) as this may reduce their vitality. On the other hand, demanding species such as pampas grass (*Cortaderia selloana*), porcupine grass (*Miscanthus sinensis*) and cord grass (*Spartina pectinata*) must be treated with compound fertilizer during early growth. Other attractive decorative grasses are feather grass (*Stipa gigantea* and *S. pennata*) and gardener's garters (*Phalaris arundinacea*). Cut off the inflorescences and stems which are not very decorative after wilting. Leave the decorative inflorescences (if these are not required for dried flower arrangements) on the plants until spring. Then, just before sprouting, cut them off with the leaves. Spring cutting is particularly important for species with thick hollow stems. If cut in autumn, water could enter the stems in winter and cause the plants to rot.

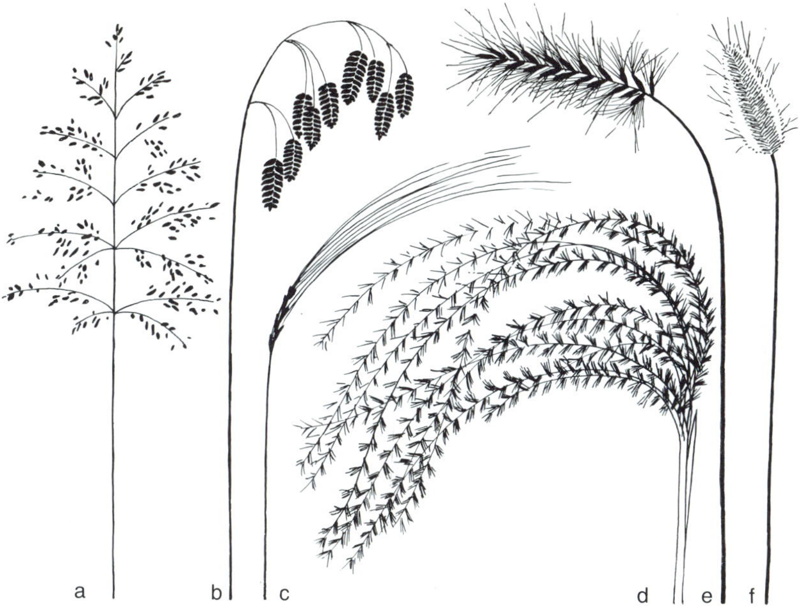

Decorative grasses with flowers of various sizes and shapes: (a) tufted hair grass (*Deschampsia caespitosa*); (b) quaking grass (*Briza media*); (c) feather grass (*Stipa pennata*); (d) porcupine grass (*Miscanthus sinensis* 'Silver Feather'); (e) feathertop (*Pennisetum villosum*); (f) hare's tail grass (*Lagurus ovatus*).

32 Creating a Grass-Based Corner of the Garden

The basis of this kind of scheme is a carpet of low-growing grasses of different colours. Fescue grass (*Festuca*) and sedge (*Carex*) are the most suitable grasses; pick those species best suited for the site in terms of soil and winter moisture, and which, since their foliage lasts through the winter, harmonize well in colour. Into this carpet plant, individually or in smaller clumps, taller grasses of varying height.

●

The best are those with interesting leaf colours, such as wild oat (*Helictotrichon sempervirens*), porcupine grass (*Miscanthus sinensis* 'Variegatus', with green and yellow leaves, and *M. s.* 'Zebrinus' with yellow cross stripes), prairie cord grass (*Spartina pectinata* 'Aureomarginata'), and oat grass (*Arrhenatherum elatius* 'Variegatum'), or those with especially decorative inflorescences such as pampas grass (*Cordateria selloana*), proso (*Panicum virgatum*), fountain grass (*Pennisetum setaceum*), and feather grass (*Stipa barbata* and *S. pennata*). Mix the grasses so that the autumn colours of each stands out.

◄ A dry rock-garden area with silver pampas grass (*Cortaderia selloana*).

Some grasses sprout later in spring than others, so enliven those temporarily empty places in your scheme with spring bulbs and some spring-flowering perennials such as *Adonis* and *Pulsatilla.* Lilies are suitable for brightening up the plot in summer, while in autumn this can be done by planting *Aster amellus* and *A. linosyris,* stonecrop (*Sedum telephium*), autumn crocuses (*Colchicum*) and so on. At the back of grassy plots plant shrubs that bear coloured fruits in autumn such as *Arbutus unedo, Pyracantha, Berberis rubrostilla, Cotoneaster, Rosa moyesii* and *R. rugosa, Skimmia japonica,* and the guelder rose *(Viburnum opulus*).

An informal scheme using creeping perennials:

(1) speedwell (*Veronica armena*); (2) stonecrop (*Sedum kamtschaticum*); (3) snow-in-summer (*Cerastium tomentosum*); (4) *Antennaria dioica;* (5) wild thyme (*Thymus praecox* ssp. *arcticus*); (6) golden marguerite (*Anthemis biebersteiniana*). Tufted low perennials: (7) *Adonis vernalis;* (8) bearded dwarf iris (*Iris pumila*); (9) *Pulsatilla grandis;* (10) eryngo (*Eryngium alpinum*). High and medium-high perennials: (11) baby's breath (*Gypsophila paniculata*); (12) sage (*Salvia* x *superba*); (13) mullein (*Verbascum olympicum*); (14) yucca (*Yucca filamentosa*); (15) stonecrop (*Sedum telephium*). Grasses: (16) wild oat (*Helictotrichon sempervirens*); (17) feathertop (*Pennisetum alopecuroides*); (18) fescue grass (*Festuca cinerea*); (19) feather grass (*Stipa pennata*); (20) purple moor grass (*Molinia caerulea*); (21) reed grass (*Calamagrostis arundinacea*); (22) fescue grass (*Festuca mairei*). Bulbs: (23) crocus (*Crocus chrysanthus*); (24) tulip (*Tulipa kaufmanniana*); (25) allium (*Allium moly*); (26) allium (*Allium karataviense*); (27) allium (*Allium albopilosum*); (28) foxtail lily (*Eremurus stenophyllus bungei*); (29) crocus (*Crocus heuffelianus*). (30) Path of stone slabs.

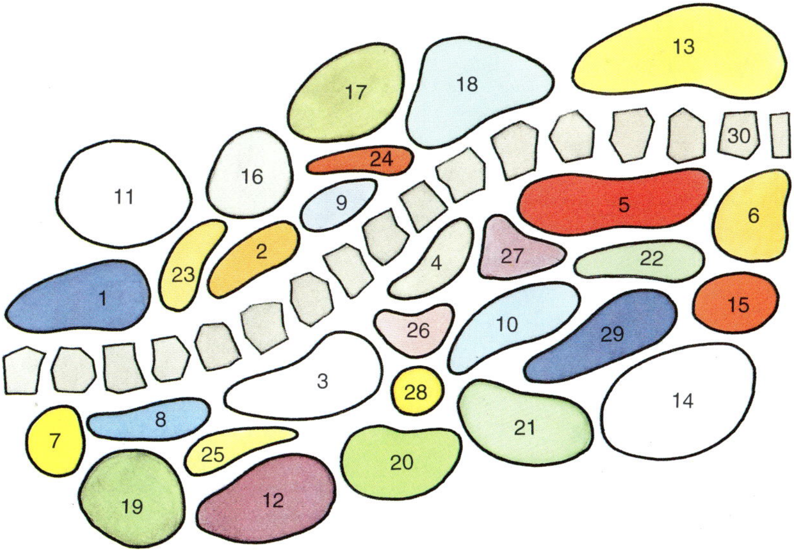

33 Grasses: Choosing the Most Decorative Forms

Fescue grass (*Festuca glauca*) is particularly suitable for well-drained, sunny banks and borders, where it forms 15—23 cm (6—9 in) clumps of bristle-like blue-grey leaves. Small purple flower spikes appear in June and July. Sheep's fescue (*F. ovina*) is also suitable for a semi-shaded site; it bears fine green to greyish-green foliage. Plant the lower-growing *F. glacialis* in rockeries, where it forms little tufts of fine silvery blue leaves. Blue-grey flower panicles, no more than 4 cm (1 $^1/_2$ in) long, appear mid-summer. Cut the dying flowerheads off fescue grasses before they shed their seeds. Lift and divide the crowns every other year and replant.

Common quaking grass (*Briza media*) grows 30—45 cm (12—18 in) tall stems and bears panicles of small purple-brown, heart-shaped flowers from late spring to the end of summer. It grows well on sunny to semi-shaded sites in well-drained soil. Propagate by dividing the crowns and seeds. Pearl grass (*B. maxima*) is an annual species; slightly taller, it bears attractive pendent, deep yellow spikelets in May—July.

The feather grasses (*Stipa*) are among the loveliest of the medium-tall grasses, with garden species varying in height from 60—120 cm (2—4 ft). The slender, usually arching stems bear long feathery plumes throughout the summer. They require a sunny site with free-draining, limy soil and protection against winter damp. Propagate in autumn from seeds or in spring by dividing the crowns. The feather grasses look especially attractive against a background of darker woody plants.

The wild oat (*Helictotrichon sempervirens*) forms dense tufts of slender, bluish-green leaves up to 45 cm (18 in) high and wide, from which rise slender, 120 cm (4 ft) high stems bearing drooping pale yellow spikes in June—July. It requires a sunny site with light, free-draining soil. Propagate by dividing the crowns.

Feathertop (*Pennisetum alopecuroides*) makes a fine specimen plant. It forms a dense clump of grey-green leaves about 45 cm (18 in) long. In September and October it produces long plumes of furry, pink-brown spikes. The species is not fully hardy and must have a sunny, sheltered site and protection in winter. Propagate by dividing the crowns or from seeds.

The queen among grasses is silver pampas grass (*Cortaderia selloana*). Up to 275 cm (9 ft) high stems terminating in long silvery plumes arise from a 1 m (3 ft) high crown of grey-green, razor-edged leaves at the end of summer. There are several varieties of *C. selloana.* 'Pumila', rarely more than 180 cm (6 ft) tall, is suitable for smaller gardens; 'Rosea' has pinkish-silver plumes; 'Gold Band' and 'Silver Comet' have striped leaves. Pampas grass needs well-drained, fertile soil in full sun and protection from north winds. In winter it requires protection against frost and damp. Propagate by division and plant as a solitary specimen in island beds.

The type species of porcupine grass (*Miscanthus sinensis*) rarely flowers in the garden, so choose one of the many beautiful cultivars: the lower-growing 'Gracillimus', with its lovely sage-green leaves (see the picture at left); 'Silver Feather', with beautiful silky plumes in autumn; 'Variegatus', with green and yellow foliage; and 'Zebrinus', whose transverse gold bars on the leaves remind one of a delicate bamboo plant. Porcupine grass is propagated by dividing the crowns and is best grown as a solitary plant. Cut off the dead stems at ground level in March before new shoots arise. Plant in March or April on a sunny site in moist garden soil.

A selection of low and medium high grasses: (a) fescue (*Festuca glauca*); (b) quaking grass (*Briza media*); (c) feather grass (*Stipa pennata*); (d) feathertop (*Pennisetum alopecuroides*); (e) squirrel-tail grass (*Hordeum jubatum*).

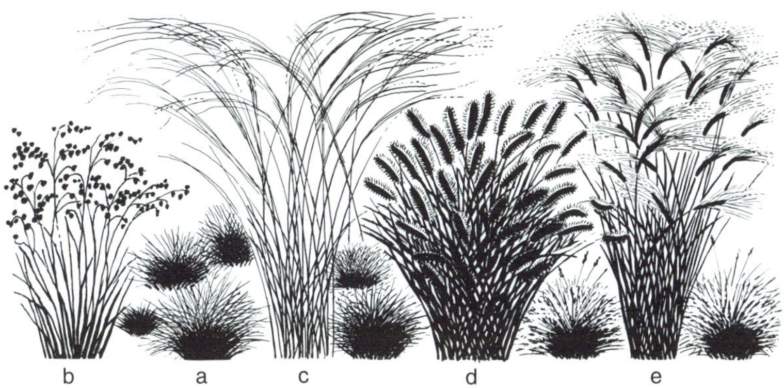

34 Siting Your Ferns

In gardens, ferns, which are mostly native to the tropics, thrive best in semi-shady and shady nooks or beneath the canopies of trees. Most of them like damp but free-draining, fertile soil. Prepare normal garden soil for ferns by mixing in a good quantity of well-decomposed leaf mould and coarse sand. Plant smaller species of rock ferns which tolerate part sunlight in rockeries where the boulders provide them with enough shade. The soil surface should be mulched with a layer of leaves to prevent evaporation of moisture and to maintain soil temperature in times of frost.

The taller, more decorative ferns can be used as specimen plants to draw the eye. But, in general, ferns perhaps are best used to set off the colour of flowers and foliage of annuals, perennials and shrubs. Many low-growing species also make excellent evergreen ground cover, while others like to luxuriate by the damp margins of a garden pond or stream.

One of the most beautiful of the taller species is the royal fern (*Osmunda regalis*), which may attain a height of 1.5 m (5 ft). The leaves are lanceolate and bipinnate and pea-green in colour. The fertile inner leaves are covered with spore capsules along their veins. The royal fern is a long-liver, and with age forms a massive clump of crowns and roots above the soil surface. *O. r.* 'Purpurascens', a somewhat lower-growing cultivar, has copper-pink young fronds that later turn copper-green.

Among the most charming of the low-growing species is the soft shield fern (*Polystichum setiferum*), particularly its cultivar 'Plumoso-divisilobum', which is 30—60 cm (1—2 ft) high with very finely divided leaves that remain green in winter. Both the species and its cultivar are planted in April in well-shaded, humous, moist, preferably alkaline soil.

Three of the finest medium-tall ferns with finely divided leaves are the lady fern (*Athyrium filix-femina*), especially its cultivar 'Victoriae', the male fern (*Dryopteris filix-mas*) and the ostrich-feather fern (*Matteucia struthiopteris*). Their infertile leaves die in autumn, but their fertile ones last through the winter. The ostrich-feather fern tends to develop extensive underground roots, and individuals should be planted at least 90 cm (3 ft) apart. Athyriums and, especially, Matteuccias, require rich, moisture-retentive soil.

Among the rarest garden ferns is the hart's-tongue fern (*Asplenium scolopendrilum,* syn. *Phyllitis scolopendrium*). It has entire, 30—45 cm (12—18 in) long leaves which stay green in winter. It grows best in damp soil containing calcium and beech-leaf mould.

Small ferns especially suitable for rockeries and dry walls include maidenhair spleenwort (*Asplenium trichomanes*), the rusty back fern *Ceterach* (often sold as a herb), and *Woodsia.*

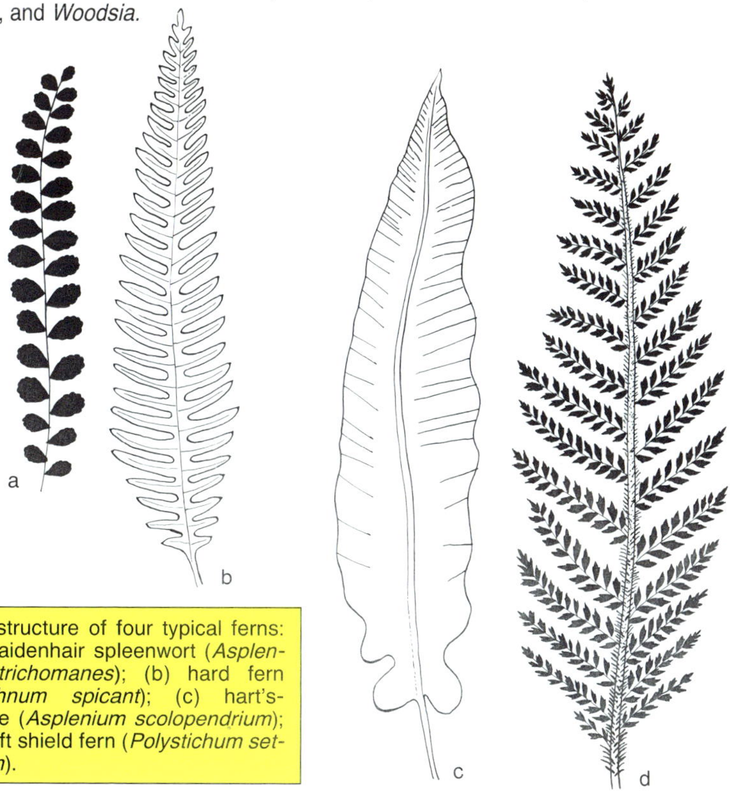

Leaf structure of four typical ferns: (a) maidenhair spleenwort (*Asplenium trichomanes*); (b) hard fern (*Blechnum spicant*); (c) hart's-tongue (*Asplenium scolopendrium*); (d) soft shield fern (*Polystichum setiferum*).

35 Heath and Heather Gardens

Heaths (mainly *Erica* species) and heathers (*Calluna*) for garden use are evergreen shrubs whose attractive foliage contributes year-round colour to the garden; in addition, the small flowers of many species remain in bloom for many months. So wide is the colour range of these shrubs that you can devote entire borders to them; or you can use them for, say, edging a path or wall, or in rockeries, or as decorative ground cover; some can even be used to make hedges.

●

Most heaths and heathers thrive best in peat-rich acid soils, though many will tolerate neutral ones, and many of the most popular winter-flowering ericas are quite happy in slightly alkaline soils. However, it is good policy to dig acid peat into the soil while preparing the ground for planting. The plants do not thrive in heavy soil, so lighten it if necessary with sharp sand and, if available, hop manure. Once the plants are established, give the soil a top-dressing of peat once a year to help it conserve moisture.

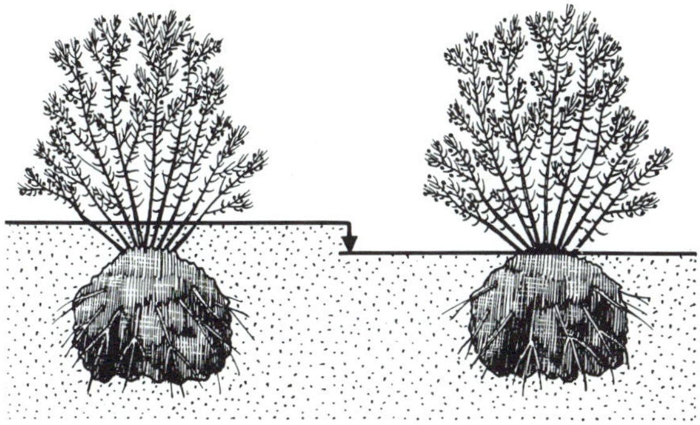

In a newly prepared heath bed, insert the plants deeper than normal so that they will be at the correct depth after the substrate has settled.

Heaths and heathers are planted either in October-November or in March—May. During the first year of growth ensure that the soil is kept moist, and water thoroughly during dry spells. The plants should be arranged in informal groups of five or six individuals; the smaller varieties about 30 cm (12 in) apart, the larger ones 45 cm (18 in) apart. Propagate heaths and heathers by cuttings of side-shoots taken from July to October. The cuttings should be grown in a mist propagator in a mixture of two parts of sharp sand to one part of acid peat.

If you need to limit the size of your heaths and heathers, trim the stems to unequal lengths (left-hand drawing), otherwise the shrubs will acquire unnaturally uniform shapes.

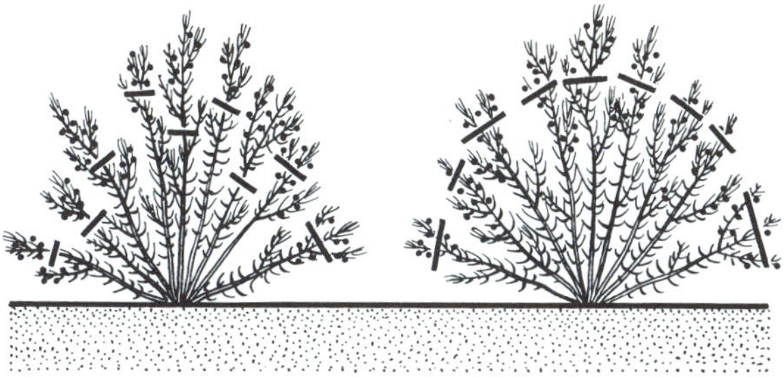

36 Choosing Heaths and Heathers

The red winter-flowering heath (*Erica herbacea,* syn. *E. carnea*), its hybrid *E.* x *darleyensis* and their many cultivars flower from late autumn until May or June, producing white, gold, pink, rose-purple and carmine blooms. Then, for the second half of the year, you can combine common heather or ling (*Calluna vulgaris*) with bell heather (*Erica cinerea*), cornish heath (*E. vagans*) and cross-leaved heath (*E. tetralix*). All these species, too, have numerous cultivars that bear white, pink, red or violet flowers. Most, like the winter bloomers, are rarely taller than 60 cm (2 ft), though *E. vagans* may attain 1.2 m (4 ft) and spread 2.4 m (8 ft) and more. Clip plants flowering in autumn after they wilt, and shorten plants flowering in summer at the beginning of spring of the following year. Trim cultivars with multicoloured leaves and finely branched stems in the second half of August. Trim only the tips of the stems of the slow growers, but prune rampant heathers by a third of their length.

As we have seen (Hint 34), propagation is by side-shoot cuttings. Place the boxes and pots containing the cuttings under glass or plastic foil. Keep the air temperature at 15°C (59°F) at least and the sharp sand/acid peat

◀ Hardy evergreen staples of the heath garden.

Heathers and heaths can be propagated by layering in spring or from cuttings taken from midsummer to the middle of autumn.

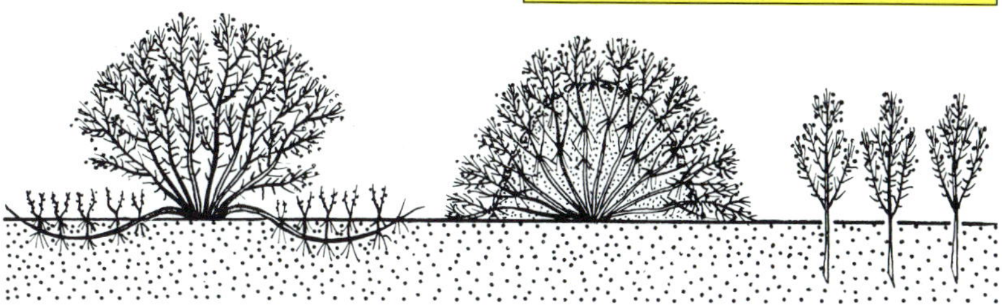

growing medium adequately damp during rooting. Grow the rooted cuttings in a cold frame or unheated greenhouse, and plant them out in the garden when they are about 7.5 cm (3 in) high.

Complement your heath and heather plantings with low-growing or small weeping evergreen rhododendrons and other heath plants such as bog rosemary (*Andromeda*), *Cassiope* garden hybrids, St Dabeoc's heath (*Daboecia cantabrica*), *Gaultheria,* calico bush (*Kalmia latifolia*), and Labrador tea (*Ledum groenlandicum*). Small bulbs and tuberous flowering plants of inconspicuous colour, low and medium-high grasses, prostrate conifers and deciduous shrubs are also suitable, while ferns can be planted in shady areas.

An irregularly planted heath garden flowering throughout the year.

Heaths: (1) *Erica herbacea* (syn. *E. carnea*) 'Alba'; (2) *E. herbacea* 'Praecox Rubra'; (3) *E. herbacea* 'Aurea'; (4) bell heather (*E. cinerea* 'Rosea'); (5) Cornish heath (*E. vagans* 'Rubra'). Heathers: (6) *Calluna vulgaris* 'Alba Plena'; (7) *C. vulgaris* 'J. H. Hamilton'; (8) *C. vulgaris* 'Cuprea'; (9) *C. vulgaris* 'Alportii Praecox'. Perennials: (10) catmint (*Nepeta* x *faassenii*); (11) burning bush (*Dictamnus albus*); (12) alyssum (*Alyssum montanum*); (13) *Paronychia serpyllifolia;* (14) candytuft (*Iberis saxatilis*); (15) stonecrop (*Sedum spectabile*); (16) fescue grass (*Festuca glauca*). (17) Decorative bush plants.

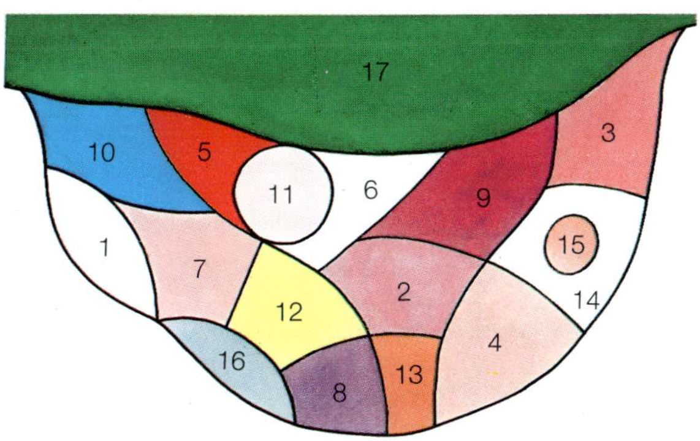

37 Making a Garden Pond

An ornamental pool should reflect, in its shape and size, the character and size of the garden and species of plants grown there. A regularly shaped pool — a rectangle, square or perfect circle — looks best in a formal garden, while freer shapes are appropriate in a more informal setting. Try to site your pool away from trees. Shady areas are unsuitable, and in any case leaves blown into the water not only present a tedious cleaning problem but may release gases in the water that are poisonous to fish and other pond animals.

Concrete pools, if built well, last a long time, but they involve a lot of work, including the use of shuttering (timber forms to hold the concrete to the required shapes while it sets). Today the commonest materials are glass-fibre set into pre-formed shapes. They are restricted in size and quite expensive, but are easy to instal. Vacuum-formed pools are similar in appearance; they are cheaper but also more fragile. The best materials for the typical modern pool are flexible liners, which are available in polythene, laminated PVC, and butyl rubber. Polythene is cheapest and least durable; butyl rubber is the toughest and most expensive. For most do-it-yourself pool projects, laminated PVC is the best bet.

Once you have decided on the size and shape of the pond, you can work out the area of liner required by taking the greatest length and multiplying it by the greatest width after adding twice the total depth to each of these measurements. You can create a balanced environment for plants and fish by providing space for shallow- and deep-water plants. The way to achieve this is to create a 'shelf' around the edge of the pool on which to place pond baskets in which the shallow-water varieties are grown. The shelf should be about 23 cm (9 in) below the water surface and about 23 cm (9 in) wide. The depth of the pond where you will want to grow water lilies and other deep-water plants need be no more than 60 cm (2 ft).

Mark out the shape of the pool and the surrounding coping. Now dig out the whole area to a depth of 23 cm (9 in). The sides should be about 20 degrees from the vertical. Mark out the width of the marginal shelf, then dig out the remaining area to a depth of 60 cm (2 ft), again sloping the walls of the deep area. Next, remove any sharp stones from the bottom and sides and cover all the interior surfaces with a 25 mm (1 in) layer of damp soft sand. Place the liner in position and weight down the edges with bricks. Now run water into the pool to mould the liner to the shape of the dug-out area. When the pool is full, trim the liner to size, slitting any wrinkled edges, so that a 23 cm (9 in) border is left around the edge of the pool. Finally, cover this border liner with coping (stone or concrete slabs) laid on a bed of mortar.

◄ The 'Zebrinus' cultivar of the bulrush *Schoenoplectus tabernaemontani,* with its stems vividly banded in green and white, creates a fine decorative effect in the margins of a sheltered pool.

An ornamental pool built with the use of a laminated PVC liner. The liner is kept in place with stone coping around the pool margin. The dug out area must be cleared of stones and covered with a 2.5 cm (1 in) layer of soft sand.

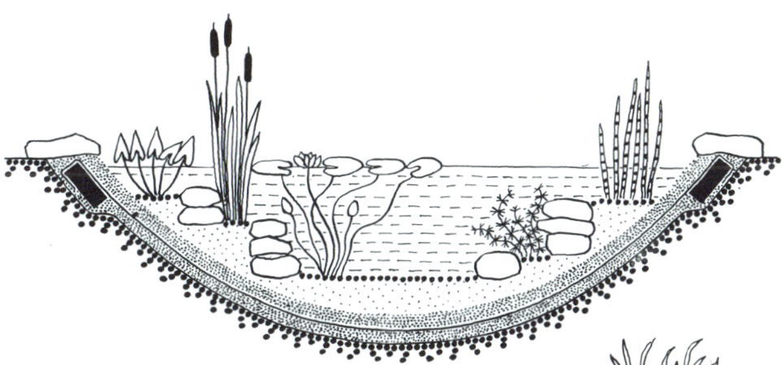

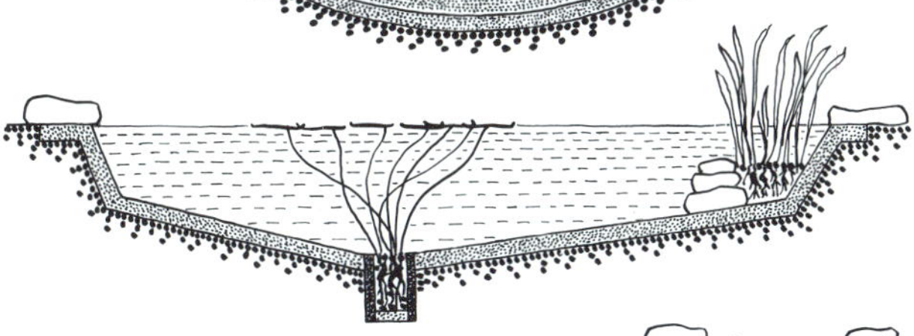

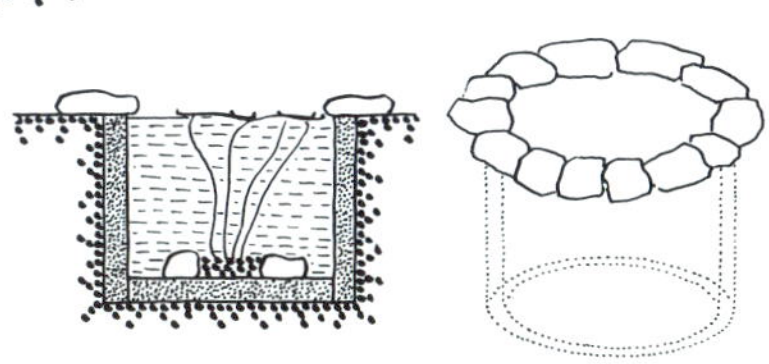

A decorative pond and a small pond with concrete walls and bottom.

38 Choosing Plants for the Pond

Water-lilies (*Nymphaea*) are the best-known and most popular garden water plants, but it is important to select those forms that are suitable for the size and depth of your pond. Among the best for small to medium-sized ponds are the hardy hybrids, most of which will grow happily in a water depth of 60 cm (2 ft) or less. Examples include 'Conqueror' (crimson flowers), 'Escarboucle' (brilliant red), 'Firecrest' (pink), 'Froebelii' (wine-red), 'James Brydon' (crimson), *N.* x *laydekeri* and its varieties (rose, pink or crimson), *N.* x *marliacea* and its varieties (white, cream or yellow), and 'Sunrise' (deep yellow).

●

In a small or medium-sized pond, it is best to grow plants in purpose-built basket-type containers you can buy at garden stores that specialise in water plants. Water lilies are planted, in their baskets, in good fertile, loamy soil in April to June. The depth of soil in the baskets should be 15—20 cm (6—8 in) for medium-sized plants and 10—15 cm (4—6 in) for small ones. Soak the soil before planting. Make sure that the crown tips are just above the soil surface.

◀ Water-lilies (*Nymphaea*) are among the finest ornamental plants for garden pools.

Place pickerel weed (*Pontederia cordata*) in a pot at a depth of 30 cm (12 in). It is sensitive to frost, so transfer it to deeper water for the winter.

Ornamental water plants for shallow planting on the marginal shelf include marsh marigold (*Caltha palustris*), water violet (*Hottonia palustris*), *Iris kaempferi,* yellow flag (*I. pseudacorus*), golden club (*Orontium aquaticum*), pickerel weed (*Pontederia cordata*), common arrowhead (*Sagittaria sagittifolia*), and sweet flag (*Acorus calamus* 'Variegatus').

Other ornamentals, for planting in deeper water, include the brandy bottle (*Nuphar lutea*), with yellow flowers in May to August; the blue-flowering floating water hyacinth (*Eichhornia crassipes*), which is not fully hardy and should be lifted and stored in winter; and Cape pond weed (*Aponogeton distachyos*).

Finally, be sure to plant a few water-oxygenating species: they keep the water clear, reduce the amount of algae on the water surface, and maintain the level of oxygen needed by other plants, fish and other animals. Oxygenators include Canadian pondweed (*Elodea canadensis*), the less vigorous *Egeria densa,* which is better for small ponds, and water milfoil (*Myriophyllum spicatum*), which has attractive feathery foliage. These plants live almost entirely submerged.

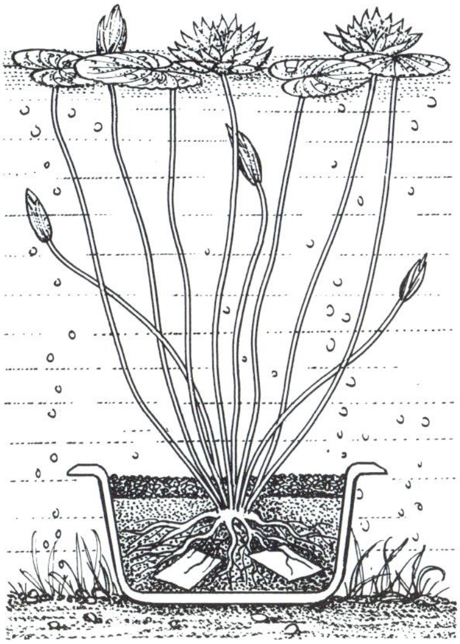

Plant water-lilies in perforated containers filled with 10–30 cm (4 to 12 in) of soil, depending on the final size of the plants. The tubers or rhizomes, planted in April–June, should have their growing point level with the soil surface. If planting established plants, enclose the roots in small water-permeable bags containing fertilizer.

39 Using Running Water

If you are lucky enough to have a stream running through your garden, there are many ways of exploiting it. You could, for instance, create a pool with aquatic plants or a small bathing pool for children by tapping the continuous supply of water. Use laminated PVC (see Hint 37) to line the pond or pool.

•

If the stream bed is on a pronounced incline, you can create the appearance and sound of rapids by installing 'steps' and placing large boulders at intervals. If the slope is even greater, throw a mini-dam across the stream, using natural stone bedded into a concrete base, to create a waterfall.

•

As with the garden pond, place coping stones or slabs around the edges of the pool, interspersing them with aquatic and bog plants such as queen of the prairie (*Filipendula rubra*), monkey flower (*Mimulus cardialis*), bog arum

◄ Flowering plants around a brook.

(*Calla palustris*), Japanese primrose (*Primula japonica*), bog bean (*Menyanthes trifoliata*), water forget-me-not (*Myosotis palustris*), *Iris pseudacorus,* purple loosestrife (*Lythrum salicaria*), and creeping jenny (*Lysimachia nummularia*). It is vital, however, that these plants are sited in soil that is permanently moist. If necessary, hose the soil thoroughly in dry weather, and mulch the surface with peat.

●

There are many other plants that, although not bog plants or aquatics, thrive in moist soil. These include *Astilbe, Hosta, Iris kaempferi, Iris sibirica,* the globeflower (*Trollius*), spiderwort (*Tradescantia* x *andersoniana*), several primroses including drumstick primrose (*Primula denticulata*) and *P. sieboldii,* and tall perennials such as goat's beard (*Aruncus dioicus*), bugbane (*Cimicifuga*), and *Ligularia tangutica,* all of which also need full sun.

The marsh marigold or kingcup (*Caltha palustris*) is one of the most suitable plants for damp soil.

Reduce the steepness of the slope of a water course by 'stepping' it with large stones or boulders (a). Install a large, flat stone or a flag at the base of a waterfall (b).

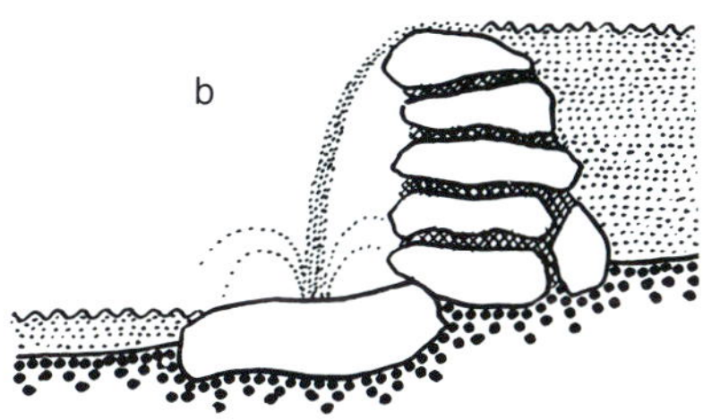

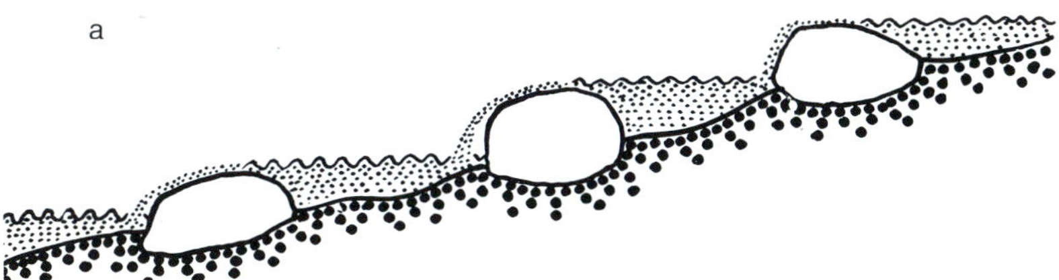

40 Making the Most of Bulbs and Tubers

Bulbs and tubers can be planted on their own in clumps, but they usually look their best if planted in association with other decorative plants such as annuals, perennials and shrubs. When planning such associations, compare the size, shape, flowering season and other features (such as autumn berries or leaf colours) of each species you plan to include in your scheme. Species flowering in spring can also be mixed with biennials flowering at the same time.

Clumps of bulbs planted on the margins of a lawn and alongside paths can look especially effective. To brighten up a regularly mown lawn with bulbs, remove the turf from several suitable places, and, after preparing the soil by hoeing and composting, plant several bulbs in each place. In general, it is best to plant an odd number of bulbs — say five or seven — at each site. Bear in mind that you will have to mow around these clumps even after the flowers die: until the foliage loses its colour and collapses it will continue to produce food that will be stored in the bulb until new shoots arise the following season. Taller plants, such as lilies, dahlias, fritillaries and cannas, can be planted as solitary specimen plants in the border. Small species are suitable for

◄ A clump of tulips planted informally in an orchard.

rockeries and for raising in small decorative pots. After early-flowering bulbs in the border die back they can be replaced for the rest of the season with bedding plants — tender or half-hardy annuals and biennials, and also those relatively short-lived, half-hardy perennials that are usually grown as annuals. If you are especially keen on cut-flowers, do not grow them in the most visible part of the decorative garden, otherwise you will be faced, at the height of the growing season, with large areas of border full of plants with cut stems. So favourites such as gladioli, daffodils (*Narcissus*) and tulips grown for cutting should be raised elsewhere in the garden.

●

In selecting a site for bulbous and tuberous plants, bear in mind that most species thrive on sunny sites, sheltered from strong winds that would dry them out. Some species, such as tuberous begonias (*Begonia* x *tuberhybrida*), cyclamens (*Cyclamen*) and certain lilies prefer semi-shaded sites.

Bulbous and tuberous flowers like light to medium heavy, well-drained, humus- and nutrient-rich soil, moist but not over-wet. The autumn crocus (*Colchicum*) tolerates damper, and the alliums drier, soil than most bulbs. The soil should be neutral to slightly alkaline. Bulbous and tuberous flowers do not tolerate soil treated with incompletely rotted manure or other organic substances, but they will benefit from the addition of alkalized peat.

Bulbs and tubers after a wide choice of tall-growing plants.

41 Planting and Caring for Bulbs and Tubers

Hoe and enrich the soil with multi-element fertilizer to a depth of 20—25 cm (8—10 in) about 14 days before planting. Add 100 g ($^1/_4$ lb) of fertilizer per square metre for species with a short growing season and about half that amount for species with a long growing season, adding the other half at the end of the season.

As a rough guide, plant bulbs and tubers so that the depth of the soil above them is three times their height; this applies to light and heavy soils alike. Water the bulbs thoroughly after planting.

Feed sprouting plants in spring with nitrate of potash (available as a liquid feed) and species with a long growing season — for instance lilies, gladiolus, and dahlias — before flowering with 50 g (2 oz) of multi-element fertilizer to the square metre. At the end of the season, bulbs and tubers of winter-hardy species remain in the ground. Lift those bulbs and tubers endangered by frost at the end of the season and dry and store them until the following spring. If the plants remain on one site for several years, improve the soil with good garden compost in the autumn. Scatter the compost on the surface; do not work it into the soil unless your bulbs are at a safe depth. The bulbs of hyacinths and certain tulips (such as the rock-garden favourite

Plant gladioli and other species grown for cutting in special beds, or even in the vegetable garden, so that after cutting their absence does not leave unsightly gaps in your ornamental beds and borders.

Tulipa pulchella) must be lifted every year — though some tulip species and varieties can be left in the soil for many years. Lift daffodil, lily and autumn crocus (*Colchicum*) bulbs every 3—4 years, and other species later, when flower production begins to tail off.

Remove the plants carefully from the soil with a spade. Cut off the dead stems and foliage, though leave about 10 cm (4 in) of the stem on dahlia tubers. Dry the bulbs and tubers in an airy room by placing them upside down so that any moisture in the stem bases can drain away. Most lilies, with the exception of the madonna lily (*Lilium candidum*) and its natural varieties, should not be lifted or transplanted. Once the bulbs and tubers are dry, store them according to the requirements of each species.

Planting depths for popular bulbous and tuberous plants:

(1) Madonna lily hybrids (*Lilium candidum*); (2) *Oxalis;* (3) winter aconite (*Eranthis hyemalis*); (4) foxtail lily (*Eremurus*); (5) *Iris reticulata;* (6) windflower (*Anemone coronaria*); (7) dog's-tooth violet (*Erythronium dens-canis*); (8) allium (*Allium moly*), snowdrop (*Galanthus*), English iris (*Iris anglica*), *Scilla,* striped squil (*Puschkinia scilloides*); (9) crocus (*Crocus*); *Crocosmia;* (10) snake's-head fritillary (*Fritillaria meleagris*); (11) gladiolus (*Gladiolus*); (12) other species of lily; (13) snowflake (*Leucojum*); grape hyacinth (*Muscari*); (14) tulip (*Tulipa*); quamash (*Camassia*); (15) autumn crocus (*Colchicum*); (16) hyacinth (*Hyacinthus*); (17) Dutch iris (*Iris* x *hollandica*); (18) daffodil (*Narcissus*); (19) allium (*Allium aflatunense, A. karataviense, A. albopilosum*); (20) allium (*Allium giganteum*); (21) crown imperial (*Fritillaria imperialis*); (22) summer hyacinth (*Galtonia*); (23) dahlia (*Dahlia*).

42 Propagating Bulbs and Tubers

'Bulb' and 'tuber' are two commonly used (and sometimes mis-used) terms for what are essentially modified stems that act, in part, as food-storage organs. Bulbs, for instance, consist of a short, fleshy stem which has a growing point encased in layers of thick fleshy scale leaves. New bulbs grow in the axils of these leaves, while both the flower and foliage grow from the centre of the bulb. Corms are very similar in appearance to bulbs, but are structurally different. Daffodils, tulips and lilies are typical bulbous plants; crocuses, gladioli and montbretia are familiar plants that develop corms. Tubers are swollen underground stems; typical examples are nasturtiums (*Tropaeolum*), water lilies (*Nymphaea*), and of course the potato. Rhizomes are perennial storage stems that grow horizontally, rather than vertically, at or just below the soil surface. Familiar examples of plants propagated from rhizomes are bearded irises, lily-of-the-valley (*Convallaria*), rex begonias, and peonies.

Some bulbs, notably Canada lily (*Lilium canadense*), *L. bulbiferum,* madonna lily (*L. candidum*) and tiger lily (*L. tigrinum*), produce bulblets (tiny bulbs below ground). You can artificially stimulate these species into producing bulblets in greater quantities in the following way. In summer remove the flower stem of the plant by twisting it out of the bulb. Pinch out any buds or flowers on the stem and bury two thirds of the stem horizontally in a trench about 30 cm (6 in) deep, leaving the rest sticking out of the end of the trench. Fill the trench with light compost after spraying the stem with a liquid fungicide such as benomyl. By autumn, bulblets will have developed in the leaf axils of the buried portion of stem. These can be detached and planted in their flowering position.

Many other lilies, and also fritillaries, can be propagated by bulb scaling. 'Scales' is the name given to the fleshy leaves enclosing the bulb stem of these plants. Take cuttings, preferably in autumn, from these bulbs by pressing the scale leaves outwards until they snap off near the bulb base. (If you take only a few outer scale leaves from each bulb, it can be replanted.) Treat the leaves with a fungicidal powder, then place them in a polythene bag with a mixture of damp sterile peat and grit. Seal the bag and store at a temperature of about 21°C (70°F).

After about six weeks, depending on the variety of plant, bulblets will begin to develop at the base of the scale leaf. Now take the leaves out of their bag and plant them in pots or trays containing a suitable potting compost. The leaves must be planted vertically, with their tips just visible above the compost. Keep the pots or trays in the same warm environment, with plenty of light, and water them sparingly. In spring the bulblets will grow leaves above the compost. The plants should be hardened off in the summer. Then, when the leaves die down, lift and separate the new bulbs and plant them out.

Some plants, such as *Tropaeolum,* especially the perennial *T. tuberosum,* can be propagated by dividing their tubers into two or more parts, each of which must have at least one dominant 'eye' (bud). Dust cut surfaces with a fungicide. Store the tubers in a tray at 21°C (70°F) for two or three days until they develop a protective surface layer. Now plant them out immediately at a depth of twice their own length; they rapidly produce roots and shoots. Some plants, such as gladioli, that produce large corms can be propagated by the same method. If the corms are too small to be cut up, lateral buds can be encouraged to form in the leaf axils if the main stem of the corms is removed.

Propagation of gladioli by division of tubers.

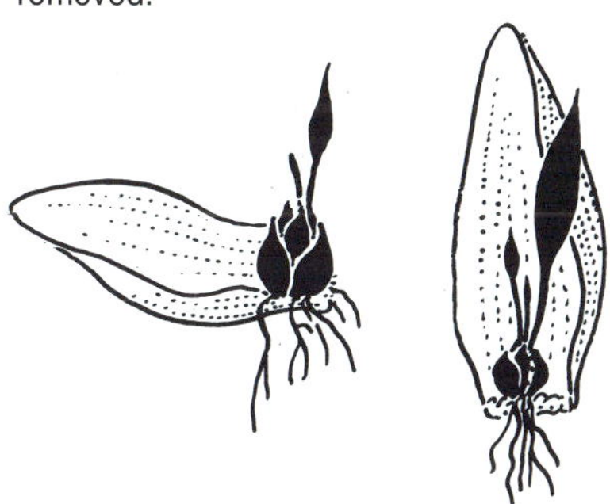

Propagation of bulbous lilies. Growing medium: (a) peat with sand, (b) garden soil, (c) peat, (d) fine gravel.

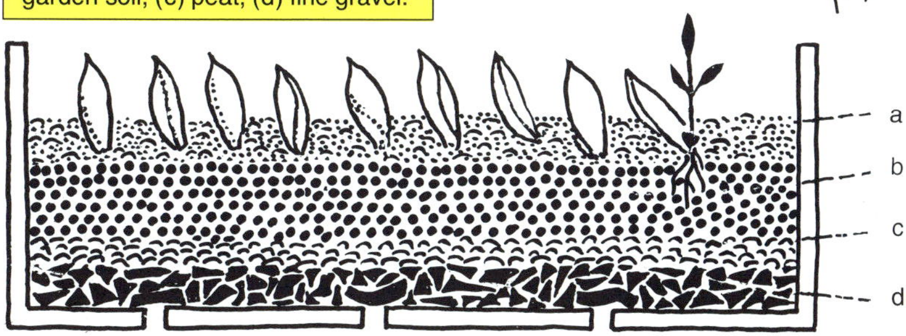

43 Success with Tulips

Massed, regimented ranks of tulips are a familiar sight in public parks and gardens. But they look best, perhaps, when grown with other bulbs, perennials, bedding plants and shrubs, where their strong colours and simplicity of outline make an important contribution to the mixed border early in the season. The 30 or so species widely available flower in March, April and May, while the hundreds of garden varieties bloom from April. The smaller species, such as *Tulipa tarda, T. pulchella* and *T. linifolia,* none of which is taller than 30 cm (6 in), look especially good at the front of rockeries, while the taller and larger-flowered species, such as *T. kaufmanniana, T. fosteriana, T. greigii, T. eichleri* and *T. tubergeniana* are used in much the same way as the garden varieties. Some species, notably *T. greigii,* have attractively veined and marbled leaves.

Plant tulips in autumn, preferably not before October or they may suffer from late-winter frosts. They thrive best in light to medium heavy, well-drained soil with a neutral or slightly alkaline reaction. Hoe the soil 14 days before planting, working in garden compost at the rate of about 5 kg (11 lb) and multi-element fertilizer at the rate of 100 g (3 $^1/_3$ oz) to the square metre. Plant the bulbs at a depth of 15—20 cm (6—8 in) — the shallow depth on heavy soils. If the tulips are to form their own informal clump, plant the bulbs 10—15 cm (4—6 in) apart depending on their size. If they are to intermingle with other spring-flowering plants, such as wall flowers (*Cheiranthus*), space them out more. The tulip species prefer full sun but the garden varieties will tolerate partial shade. Water in the bulbs thoroughly. When the tulips begin to come up in spring, feed them with a proprietary form of sulphate of potash and hoe the surface of the soil.

If the plants are being grown for cut flowers, crop them in the morning when they are still half closed. In the border, dead-head the tulips as soon as the first petals fall, removing the fallen petals, which may be disease-infected. Lift and store the bulbs when the leaves turn yellow. After removing the leaves, roots and old scale leaves, store the bulbs in trays or shallow boxes in a cool, dry place out of direct sunlight. (Some tulip species, such as *T. kaufmanniana* and its varieties, do not need to be lifted; their bulbs ripen in the soil and they will continue to bloom for many years.

●

Many garden varieties, particularly those in what are classified as the Rembrandt and Parrot divisions, have colour breaks — that is, flowers with splashes of different colours. Such breaks, perpetuated by breeders, were originally due, at least in part, to viral diseases. If any of your single-colour tulips exhibit signs of such breaks it means they have a viral disease and the whole plant should be dug up immediately and burnt. Other viral diseases, which should be treated in the same way, cause white streaks or brown spots to appear on the leaves or stems.

Tulip diseases: (a) mosaic virus, which causes colour streaks on the flowers; (b) tulip fire, caused by grey mould fungus (*Botrytis tulipae*).

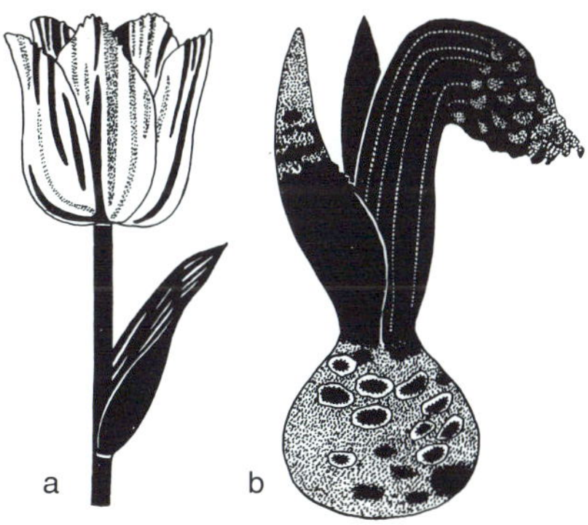

Tulips are nowadays classified into 15 divisions, based on the shape and structure of their flowers and the species from which they are derived. The four divisions represented here are: (a) Darwin, (b) Lily-flowered, (c) Parrot, and (d) Double Early.

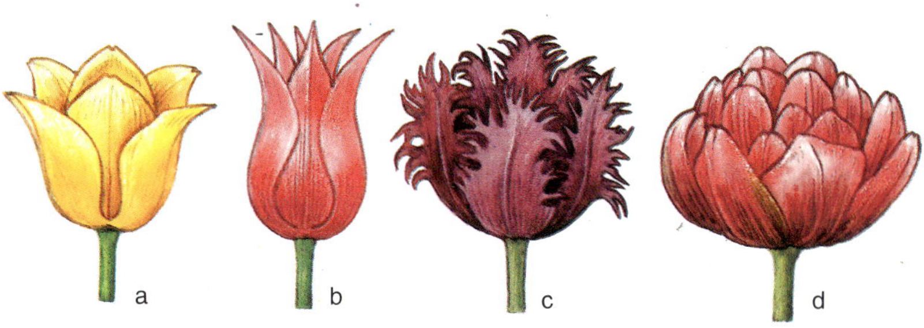

44 Growing Daffodils

All daffodils belong to the genus *Narcissus.* The terms 'daffodil' and 'narcissus' are both used as common names for these flowers, though some gardeners reserve the term 'daffodil' for those varieties in which the central trumpet-like structure of the flower is at least as long as the surrounding petals. There are more than 60 species of *Narcissus* but the great majority of daffodils grown today are selected from the many thousands of garden varieties bred from these species and grouped into a number of divisions according to their size, colour, flower shape and so on.

Daffodils flower from February to May, depending on the variety and the local climate. The flowering period for a particular variety in any one region is rarely more than two months and often less.

Daffodils can be used in formal beds or, perhaps even more attractively, in informal drifts in rough grass or on banks, in full sun or partial shade. Whichever way you prefer to use them, they fill the garden with colour before the summer-flowering perennials and shrubs come into bloom. They can also be grown under glass to provide flowers from late autumn to late spring.

If you use daffodils as bedding plants, they should be planted in the autumn and then after flowering in spring they can be lifted and replanted elsewhere in permanent sites. Those varieties in informal situations can be left undisturbed for many years. The smallest varieties, particularly suitable for rock gardens, can also be left in the ground from year to year.

Plant the bulbs in August—September in well-composted soil that has just been treated with fertilizer rich in potash and phosphate. The soil should be moist, but *not* waterlogged, at all times. Each bulb should be planted at a depth three times its own length or slightly deeper. In beds and borders they should be planted 10—20 cm (4—8 in) apart, depending on variety. For planting informally, simply scatter the bulbs at various points on the chosen site and plant them where they fall. After flowering, allow the foliage to turn yellow and die before cutting it down or lifting the bulbs. The bulbs continue to store food as long as the leaves remain green.

Sometimes daffodils become stunted and do not flower because their bulbs are eaten by the larvae of narcissus flies (*Merodon equestris*). The stricken bulbs, which are softer when pressed, and may show the entry holes of the larvae, should be removed and burned. From late April to June protect freshly planted bulbs with frequent applications of an insecticidal dust.

The narcissus fly (*Merodon equestris*) and a daffodil bulb damaged by its larvae.

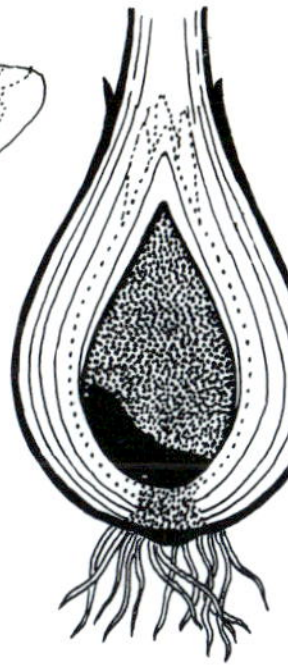

Daffodil cultivars are classified into 11 divisions, based mainly on the size and shape of the flowers. Four examples of the divisions: (a) Trumpet, (b) Short-cupped, (c) Poeticus, (d) Tazetta.

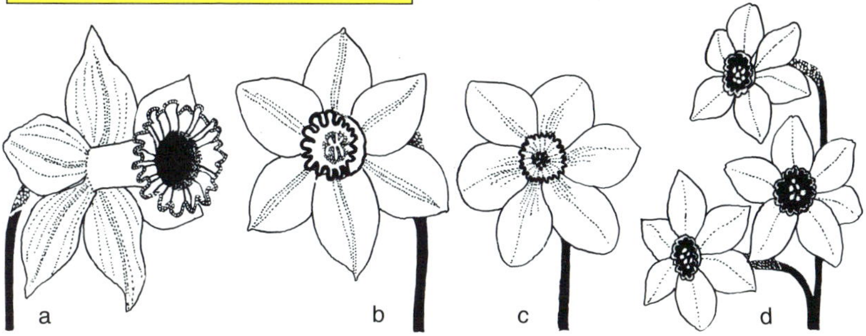

45 Spring Colour and Scent with Hyacinths

Most hyacinths grown in gardens and as houseplants derive from *Hyacinthus orientalis,* a native eastern Europe that is itself rarely available nowadays. The hybrids are commonly known as Dutch hyacinths and their flower spikes, 10—15 cm (4—6 in) long, are larger than those of the parent species. The colours of the hybrid flowers include yellow, white, pink or red, and blue. The plants are 15—23 cm (6—9 in) high. The Roman hyacinth (*H. o. albulus*) and its varieties, rarely more than 15 cm (6 in) high, make excellent rockery plants and houseplants.

For the spring border, plant hyacinth bulbs in mid-September or October on a sunny site about 15 cm (6 in) deep in light, well-drained, humous and nutritious soil that has been hoed and given a top dressing of multi-element fertilizer at the rate of 100 g (3 $^1/_2$ oz) to the square metre. The bulbs should be planted in groups of, say, five or seven; individual bulbs should be about 15 cm (6 in) apart. Water them well after planting.

Hyacinths flower in April. After the flowers fade, dig up the border hybrids and replant them in a site where they can remain indefinitely. They look particularly attractive when associated with daffodils in rough grass or under trees. When these permanently sited hyacinths fade, pull the witted flowers off the stem to prevent the formation of seeds.

If you wish to grow hyacinths as houseplants you can buy 'prepared' (specially treated) bulbs; these are now widely available in both the Dutch and Roman hyacinth varieties. Pot the bulbs in August or September and they will bloom before Christmas. Untreated bulbs potted from August to October will flower a month or two later. Both sorts of bulbs grow best in a proper potting compost. Use pots, bowls or other containers with drainage holes to ensure the bulbs do not become waterlogged. Plant the bulbs so that their 'noses' are level with the surface of the compost. Keep the bulbs moist and cool for the first six to eight weeks to encourage healthy root growth. At the end of this period, bring the containers into a light, warm position, adding progressively more heat. After they have finished flowering, the bulbs can be planted about 15 cm (6 in) deep in the garden in March and April.

To propagate hyacinths from bulbs, they need to be 'scored'. At the end of the summer, lift and clean the bulbs and cut into the bulbs' basal plates to expose the inner scale leaves. After dusting the wounds with a fungicide, place them upside down in a tray of dry sand at a room temperature of 21°C (70°F). New bulblets will develop on the site of the wounds, and, as soon as this becomes evident, plant the bulbs — still upside down — just below the surface of the compost in pots or bowls. Place them in a cold frame for the winter. In the spring, the bulblets will grow shoots and the parent bulbs will die off. The new bulbs can now be re-planted, and should flower in three or four years.

Preparing hyacinth bulbs for incubation to create bulblets: (a) cutting out basal plate, making sure that the base of every scale leaf is removed; (b) scoring — making three cuts through the basal plate. Method (b) results in fewer but larger bulblets than (a).

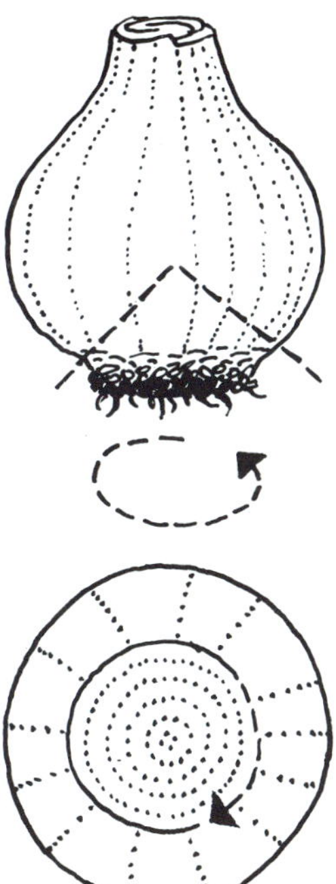

a

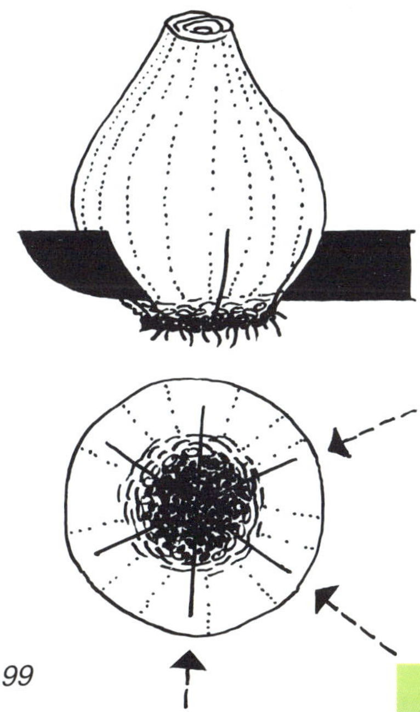

b

46 Spectacular Fritillaries

The most commonly grown fritillary species, particularly in formal beds in country gardens, is the imposing crown imperial (*Fritillaria imperialis*). In April and May its ramrod straight stem, with rising whorls of leaves, terminates in a cluster of upright leaves, beneath which tulip-shaped yellow, orange or red flowers hang in a circle around the stem.

Crown imperials can be grown in the garden either as individual specimens or in a clump with a variety of spring-flowering perennials, such as yellow leopard's bane (*Doronicum*), or in a mixed carpet of pink, red or blue *Aubrieta,* white *Arabis* and multicoloured *Alyssum* (syn. *Lobularia maritima*). It thrives best on a sunny or partly shaded site in deep, fertile, not too heavy soil. Plant bulbs from September to November to a depth of 20 cm (8 in) and 23—40 cm (9—15 in) apart. Handle the bulbs carefully: they do not like long exposure to air and are prone to bruising. The stems should be cut down in summer after the flowers have died, and the bulbs should not be transplanted for at least four years unless you wish to propagate from bulblets. The method is the same as for hyacinths (*see* Hint 44), the bulbs being lifted in June or July.

◄ Crown imperial (*Fritillaria imperialis*).

Note that the entire plant, including the bulb, is poisonous and should be handled with gloves.

The quite different, but also spectacular, snake's-head fritillary (*F. meleagris*) is suitable for semi-shaded and damp places in flower beds, rockeries, in short grass and on the edges of ponds and streams. It grows to a height of 30—45 cm (12—18 in). In May, on a thin herbaceous stem, it grows in pairs of, or single, bell-shaped flowers which have purple-chequered markings on a white background. Varieties have green-veined, greyish purple, brown-spotted, violet and other flower colours and patterns. Similar, but lower-growing, *F. latifolia* also has delightful chequered or spotted varieties.

Fritillaries can also be grown as pot plants. Plant them singly in pots in autumn under glass at a temperature of 5—7°C (41—45°F), watering them sparingly until they start to shoot.

The fritillary also has yellow-flowering cultivars.

Snake's-head fritillary (*Fritillaria meleagris*) is highly suitable for a rockery with its purple-chequered, lantern-like flowers.

Fritillaria persica, rather like a small crown imperial, flowers in late spring.

47 Choosing the Best Site for Alliums

Allium is the genus to which onions, chives and garlic belong. It also includes a number of ornamental, hardy bulbous plants that deserve a place in any garden. They like well-drained soil on a sunny site; in spring and early summer the soil should be adequately moist, so water the plants in dry spells. Later, particularly in winter, the plants require drier soil.

Most allium bulbs are frost-resistant. Plant the bulbs in September or October at a depth of about four times their own length. Allow them to grow undisturbed on one site for several years, by which time they will form clumps. When their growth becomes too dense, dig them up after the leaves turn yellow, dry and store them at a temperature of 18—20°C (64—68°F) until they are replanted. Species that grow rapidly can be divided in autumn or spring and planted in moist soil. Other species are propagated from seed and grown in pots in a cold greenhouse. The seedlings produce flower-bearing bulbs in 2—3 years.

Depending on species, alliums flower in late spring to late summer. The taller species, with their elegant globe-shaped inflorescences, look best as solitary specimens or in clumps. They associate well with dry-loving perenni-

◀ The large inflorescences of *Allium albopilosum* make a fine decoration for the garden and, after drying, for winter bouquets.

als such as the clove pink or gilliflower (*Dianthus caryophyllus*), fernleaf yarrow (*Achillea filipendulina*), golden marguerite (*Anthemis*), wild thyme (*Thymus praecox* ssp. *arcticus*), pasque flower (*Pulsatilla*), *Eryngium,* mullein (*Verbascum*), *Yucca* and sage (*Salvia nemorosa*). Grasses also make good companions, particularly fescue grass (*Festuca*), wild oat (*Helictotrichon sempervirens,* syn. *Avena sempervirens*), *Pennisetum,* and feather-grass (*Stipa*).

●

One of the most attractive decorative alliums is *A. albopilosum.* It is 30 to 45 cm (12—18 in) high and its violet-pink spherical inflorescences, 15 to 20 cm (6—8 in) in diameter, decorate the garden even when the flowers dry up. It is suitable for cutting into dry bouquets. *A. giganteum* grows to a height of 120 cm (4 ft) and has dense, perfectly spherical umbels of violet flowers up to 10 cm (4 in) wide. *A. caeruleum,* syn. *A. azureum*, is 50—60 cm (20—24 in) high and has slightly smaller umbels of azur blue flowers. Its bulbs are not altogether frost-resistant and require a cover of leaves during a spell of harsher frosts.

Plant lower-growing alliums — up to 30 cm (12 in) in height — in borders or on rockeries. The yellow *A. moly* has star-shaped flowers, *A. oreophilum var. ostrowskianum* has rose-pink flowers, and *A. karataviense* has light pink inflorescences which can be dried for winter bouquets and is also attractive for its wide bluish-green purple-edged leaves.

The flower-heads of the various decorative species of allium differ in size, structure and colour: (a) *Allium albopilosum,* (b) giant allium (*A. giganteum*), (c) yellow allium (*A. moly*), (d) *A. karataviense.*

48 Making the Most of Your Lilies

Devote great care to the selection of a site: lilies (*Lilium*) require deep, well-drained, fertile soil, rich in humus and adequately damp; they do not like heavy, wet soils. Some species and hybrids prefer lime in the soil (*L. candidum, L. martagon,* etc.); other species and hybrids do better in lime-free soil (*L. speciosum*, 'Asian Hybrids', 'Oriental Hybrids', etc.).

●

The site for lilies should be sunny or in semi-shade; they do not like the mid-day sun. Frost valleys and windy sites are also unsuitable.

●

Most lily bulbs are planted between October and March, though basal rooting types will do better if planted in the autumn. Treat the soil beforehand with multi-element fertilizer and hoe it in thoroughly. Plant the bulbs so that their tips are covered by a 8—10 cm (3—4 in) layer of earth. (An exception is *L. candidum*, which should have the tips just below the surface.)

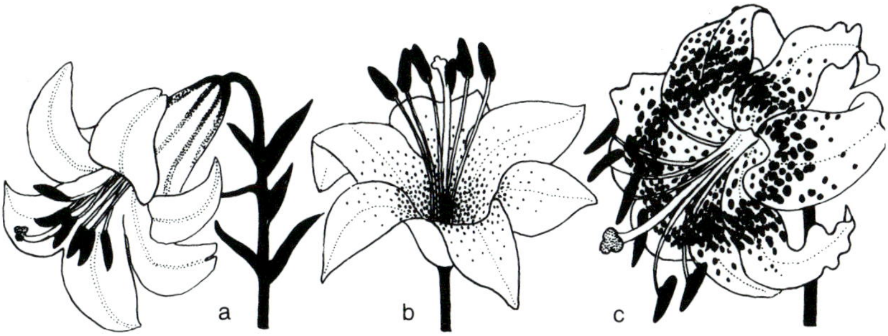

Types of lily flowers: (a) tubular, (b) bowl-shaped, (c) turban-shaped.

Before planting, remove any damaged scales and roots from the bulb and sprinkle the wounds with charcoal powder or a fungicidal agent. Sprinkle up to 5 cm of fine rubble or coarse sand around the bulb to aid rapid drainage of excess damp. Water the planted bulbs and protect the top soil against drying out with a 3 cm (1 in) layer of decomposed leaf mould or peat. In spring protect young shoots with cloches until the last frosts have gone.

●

Transplant lilies when their production of flowers begins to tail off — usually after 3—4 years. Cut flowers for the vase about 5 cm (2 in) above the ground.

●

Lilies look especially attractive if interplanted with lower-growing perennials or annuals or against a background of bushy shrubs.

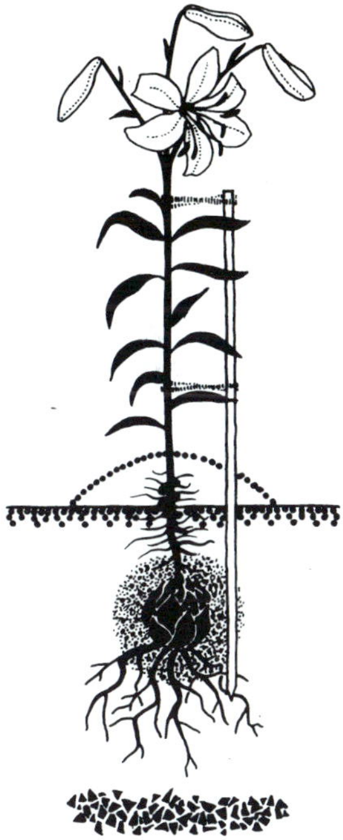

Correctly planted lily.

49 Success with Gladioli

Gladioli (*Gladiolus*) are among the most beautiful summer flowers grown mainly for cutting. In view of the fact that they are not particularly attractive when not in flower, avoid raising them in your most prominent borders; many people, in fact, grow them in the kitchen garden among vegetables.

Gladioli require a sunny site protected against wind. They like moderately heavy, *p*H neutral soil, rich in nutrients and humus. Deeply hoe a bed after applying a thin dressing of well-rotted manure, then rake in some bone meal.

Fourteen days before planting, place the gladioli corms in a warm room so they can sprout. Then plant them in prepared beds 25 cm (10 in) apart in rows 12—15 cm (5—6 in) apart and to a depth of 10 cm (4 in). In areas of higher than average rainfall, sprinkle a 2—3 cm (1—1 $^1/_2$ in) layer of sharp sand under the tubers to ensure good drainage. In order to extend the harvesting period of the cut flowers, plant the corms at three or four different times from mid-March to the end of April.

Hoe the beds after the shoots appear, and begin to water the gladioli eight to 10 weeks after planting. Feed the young shoots with potash, and later replace this with compound fertilizer. Remove diseased or stunted plants. Cut inflorescences with one or two leaves when the bottom-most flower is opening up. Cut off wilted inflorescences and remove them promptly from the bed, so that the formation of seeds is not weakened by the development of new tubers.

Gladiolus hybrids flower from July to August or September. There are four main types: large-flowered, with spikes up to 50 cm (20 in) long; Primulinus hybrids with more loosely arranged florets; miniatures with similar but somewhat smaller florets; and butterfly hybrids. All, especially the large-flowered forms, are available in hundreds of floret colours.

The development cycle of gladioli.

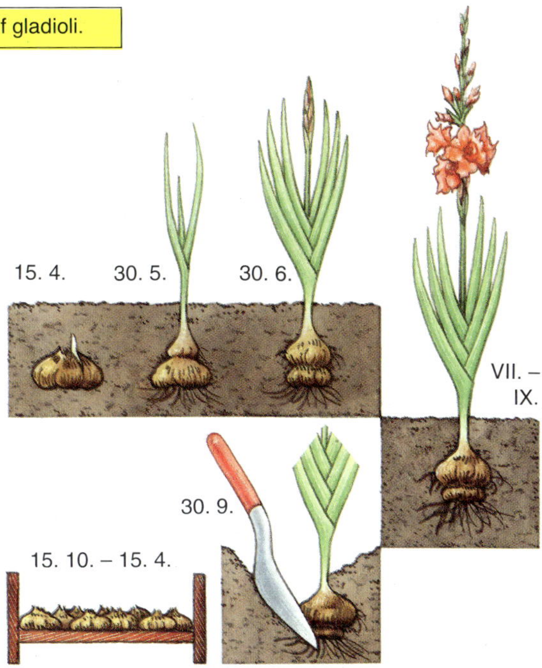

Planting gladiolus tubers with the aid of a hole cutter.

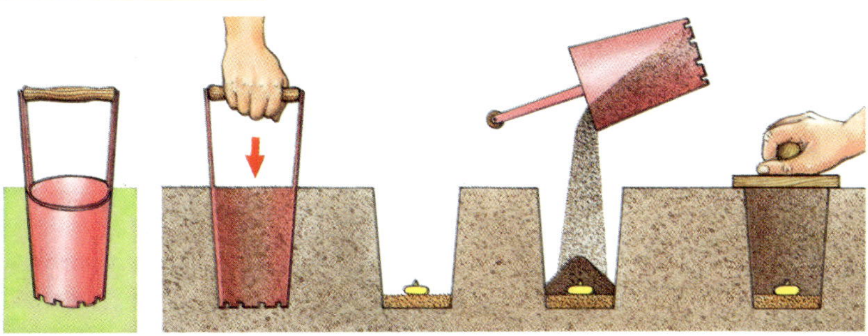

50 Keeping Gladioli Healthy

Gladioli suffer from a wide range of fungal and bacterial diseases during the growing period. Core rot (*Botrytis gladiolorum*) attacks the corms, turning them black and spongy; any shoots that may have formed will turn yellow and collapse. Less badly affected plants may develop brown spots on the leaves and flowers. Diseased plants should be destroyed. In damp conditions, corms for storage should first be submerged in benomyl solution or other suitable fungicide.

Gladiolus dry rot (*Stromatina gladioli*) kills the foliage and infects the corms, which gradually blacken. Burn all diseased corms when they are lifted and treat contaminated soil with a suitable fungicide. Corms for storage should be immersed in benomyl, as for core rot.

Gladioli are also vulnerable to cucumber mosaic, a virus spread by aphids which affects many decorative garden plants. Infected plants must be destroyed immediately and the aphids controlled with a suitable spray. The telltale signs of the virus are white blotches on the flowers and streaky marks or yellow rings on the leaves.

Gladiolus corms are not frost-resistant. Lift them in dry weather in autumn

◀ Typical signs of the gladiolus virus.

just as the stems begin to turn yellow. Gently remove all soil, and cut off the stem about 2.5 cm (1 in) above the corms. Dry the corms for a week or two, placing them on slatted shelves so that air can circulate around them. When they are thoroughly dry, store the corms in trays in a cool but frost-free place.

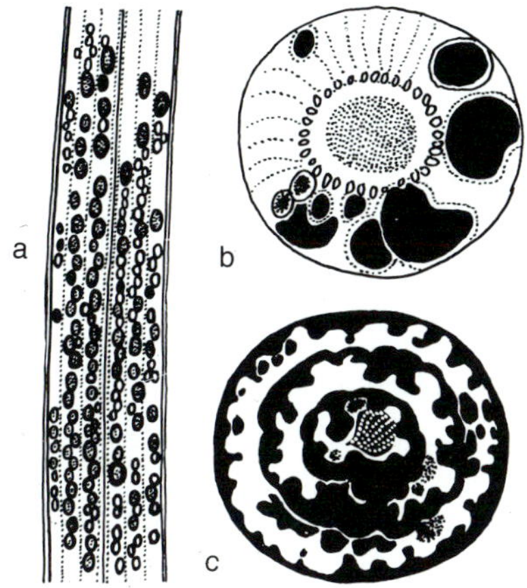

Gladiolus diseases: (a) grey mould on the leaf; (b) gladiolus scab; (c) core rot.

Discourage fungal and viral diseases by treating the corms before planting them (see Hint 8), after removing the old, toughened scale leaves. Plant the corms immediately after the treating agent dries out. If gladioli become diseased, do not plant corms in the same bed for five or six years. During the growing season spray the plants with a suitable fungicidal agent at the recommended intervals.

The most important insect pest of gladioli, apart from virus-bearing aphids, is gladiolus thrips (which also attacks crocuses and freesias). These thin, brown or yellow insects (*Taeniothrips simplex*) and their larvae suck sap from the leaves, especially in hot, dry weather, causing a silvery mottling in the foliage; the flowers may also be affected and will fail to open. Affected plants should be sprayed with fenitrothion insecticide.

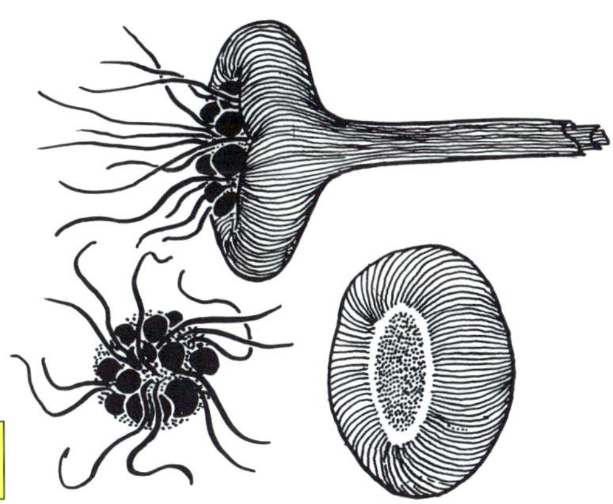

Preparing gladiolus tubers for winter.

51 Growing Tuberous Begonias

Tuberous begonias (*Begonia* x *tuberhybrida*) are 30—60 cm (12—14 in) tall tender, deciduous perennials that bear beautiful, mainly double, white, yellow, pink or red flowers, 7—15 cm (3—6 in) in diameter, from July to September. There is also a hybrid strain of *B. x tuberhybrida* listed as Pendula, with slightly smaller flowers. A further range of tuberous begonias, the result of crossing *B. x tuberhybrida* with *B. socotrana,* is known as the Elatior or Hiemalis group; these flower in December and January and are grown under glass.

●

Start the *B.* x *tuberhybrida* tubers in boxes of damp peat in March or April at a temperature of 18°C (64°F); the hollow side of the tubers should face upwards. When shoots develop leaves, transfer the plants to 12.5 cm (5 in) pots of suitable compost, potting them on in 20 cm (8 in) pots. After a further month feed them every fortnight until the end of the flowering season.

If you wish to use the begonias as bedding plants, harden them off in a cold frame in May and plant them out in June. They should be lifted in October before the early frosts. Store the tubers during winter in dry peat or clean soil at a temperature of about 7°C (45°F), occasionally sprinkling the peat with water.

The winter-flowering hybrids are best raised from cuttings, which are rooted in pots in a mixture of peat and sand at a temperature of 15°C (64°F). Pot on as necessary. After the plants are in their final pots, feed them every 10 days or so. They need light shading in a well-ventilated greenhouse during the summer, and in hot weather should be syringed with water. Support the plants with pea sticks or other canes, and pinch out the growing tips several times in early summer to encourage the plants to bush out. To delay flowering until winter, pinch out any buds that appear in September or October. During the flowering period, keep the temperature around 12°C (54°F). When the flowers fade and the leaves turn yellow, cut the plants back to about 10 cm (4 in); water them occasionally, and sparingly, and maintain the temperature at around 7°C (45°F).

Drooping tuberous begonias are especially suitable for decorative pots.

Development cycle of tuberous begonias (*Begonia* x *tuberhybrida*).

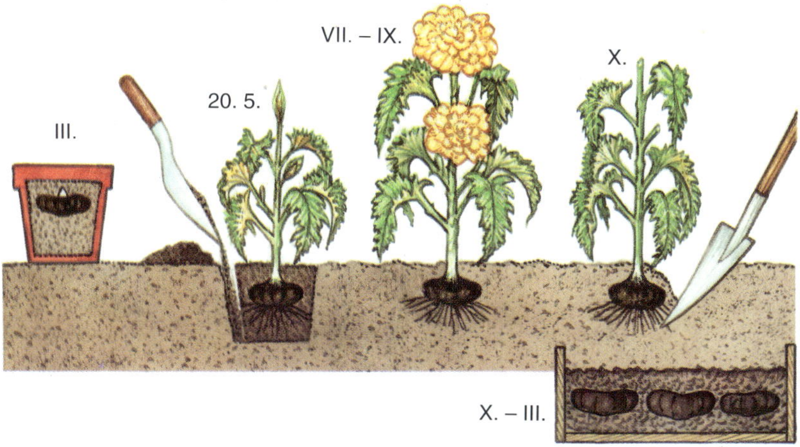

52 Dahlias: A Choice of Riches

Border dahlias, derived from three species of *Dahlia* native to Mexico, are among the most beautiful late-summer- and autumn-flowering tuberous perennials. There are hundreds of hybrids, which fall into one of the following eight groups according to the appearance, size and shape of their flowers: single-flowered, anemone-flowered, collerette, decorative, paeony-flowered, ball, pompon, and cactus. The hybrids vary greatly in height: whereas some single-flowered types are no more than 45 cm (18 in) tall, the largest hybrids in the decorative group may attain a height of 150 cm (5 ft). Again, the size of the flowers varies from group to group, from barely 5 cm (2 in) in diameter for pompons to about 25 cm (10 in) for the largest decorative ones. The colour range within each group is very great, and many blooms are bicoloured.

●

Some gardeners prefer to raise dahlias in their own beds, away from other border plants, but many of the hybrids with small to medium-sized flowers associate happily with a variety of other perennials. These include Michael-

mas daisies (*Aster novae-angliae, A. novi-belgii*), small-flowered chrysanthemums such as Shasta daisy (*Chrysanthemum maximum*), false sunflower (*Heliopsis scabra*), *Helenium autumnale* hybrids, monkshood (*Aconitum*), golden rod (*Solidago* x *hybrida*), coneflower (*Rudbeckia* x *hybrida*), and the taller grasses. A combination is also possible with decorative shrubs of vigorous growth, such as dropwort (*Filipendula vulgaris*), *Spiraea japonica,* butterfly bush (*Buddleia davidii*), *Cotoneaster,* evergreen barberries (*Berberis darwinii*) and others. Dahlias are highly suitable for cutting, which should be done when the blooms are just coming into flower; morning is the best time of day to cut them.

●

Bedding dahlias are quite distinct from the border hybrids, though they ultimately derive from the same Mexican species. They are treated as annuals and come into flower from July onwards. Rarely more than 60 cm (24 in) tall, the hybrids are available in a variety of flower forms and colours.

Dahlias are divided into several groups depending on the shape of the flowers. Four typical examples: (a) Single-flowered; (b) Decorative; (c) Pompon; (d) Cactus.

Dahlias are outstanding for their great variety of shape and colour of flowers.

53 Dahlias: Successful Cultivation

Dahlias like an open, sunny site protected from wind. The soil should be well-drained and improved with compost, peat or a little well-rotted manure. (Do not over-manure as this will promote leaf growth at the expense of flowers.) Rake in bonemeal before planting. Plant unsprouted tubers in late April and sprouted tubers or rooted cuttings in late May. Before planting, clean the tubers and soak them for 15 minutes in a solution of benomyl. (If the tubers have dried out, soak them first them for several hours in water.) Divide large clumps of tubers.

●

Plant the lower-growing hybrids 50—75 cm (20—30 in) apart and the larger ones 75—100 cm (30—40 in) apart. Dig a spacious hole for each tuber; then insert a strong cane to support the growing stem. The neck of each tuber should be about 10 cm (4 in) below the surface. Water the plants well.

Pinch out the leading shoot of each plant about a month after planting. If you are looking for large-flowered, long-stemmed plants, disbud the plants regularly by removing the two small buds that develop

A popular group of dahlias are the 'Fimbra' hybrids.

below the terminal bud on each main stem. During the growing period keep the soil adequately moist and feed the plants occasionally with a general fertilizer until the end of July.

●

Dead-head the plants promptly to encourage the formation of new buds and prolong the flowering period. After the first frosts in autumn, cut the stems down to 15 cm (6 in) in height, then gently ease the tubers out of the earth with a spade. Discard any damaged tubers, and place the remainder upside down under cover on a slatted shelf to drain any fluid from the hollow stems. After a week or 10 days, place the tubers in damp peat in shallow boxes, making sure that the peat does not cover the crowns, and store at a temperature of 4—6°C (39—43°F).

Dahlias can most easily be propagated by dividing the tubers in March. Place the tubers in shallow boxes filled with a mixture of peat and sand in equal parts, making sure that the crowns are uncovered. Store the boxes in a frost-free place; keep the growing medium moist but do not water the crowns directly. After a few weeks the 'eyes' on the crowns will swell. Divide the tubers with a sharp knife, ensuring that each segment has a healthy eye. Dust the cut areas with flowers of sulphur and plant out when ready.

Propagation of tubers through winter.

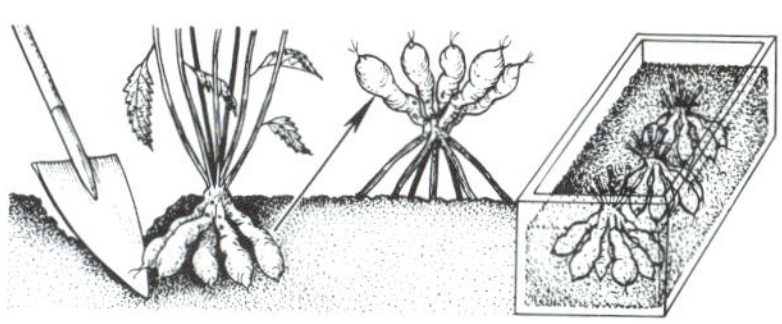

Propagating dahlias: (a) division of crowns; (b) splitting a tuber; (c) taking a cutting.

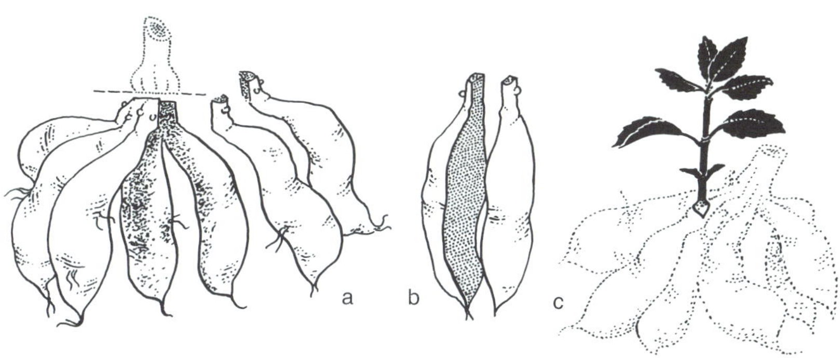

54 Two Colourful Favourites: Eremurus and Canna

Foxtail lilies (*Eremurus*) are highly decorative garden flowers. In spring they form a crown of tough, light green, strap-like leaves and in May, June or July they produce massive, superbly coloured spikes of star-shaped flowers. The largest and most commonly grown is *E. robustus,* which is 2.4—3 m (8 to 10 ft) high, with 60—120 cm (2—4 ft) long spikes of peach-yellow flowers. *E. himalaicus,* which is 1—1.5 m (3—5 ft) tall, has pure white flowers on 60 cm (2 ft) spikes. *E. stenophyllus,* syn. *E. bungei,* 1—1.2 m (3—4 ft) tall, has bright yellow flowers with orange anthers on 45 cm (18 in) spikes. *E.* 'Shelford' hybrids is a range of cultivars, 1.5—2.1 m (5—7 ft) high with 60 to 90 cm (2—3 ft) long spikes in a variety of colours from yellow to orange-buff, pink and white.

Foxtail lilies are hardy herbaceous perennials. Plant in September or October in well-drained soil in a sunny position. The crowns should be at a depth of 15 cm (6 in). They make an impressive show as specimen plants or in groups of three or five. It is a good idea to underplant the site to cover the empty spaces when the stems are cut down after the flowers fade or if, earlier still, the spikes are used as cut flowers.

◀ Planted as solitary specimen, a foxtail lily (*Eremurus stenophyllus bungei*) looks effective with its beautiful racemose flower spikes.

In spring the plants need a lot of moisture during growth, but in summer and in winter they must be watered frugally. In autumn, mulch the soil with a generous layer of old Foxtail lilies manure to protect the roots against frost.

Foxtail lilies are propagated either from seed, which should be sown as soon as they are ripe, and grown under glass at 15°C (59°F); or by dividing and replanting the roots in autumn.

●

Cannas, either Indian shot (*Canna indica*) or, more commonly, the varieties derived from *Canna* x *generalis* (syn. *C.* x *hybrida*), are tender perennials usually grown as summer bedding plants. They have large, broad leaves, either bright green or brownish purple in colour, and striking hot-red, orange, pink or bi-coloured flowers opening in mid- to late summer. The plants, which are up to 1.2 m (4 ft) high, make a fine show as individual specimens or in small clumps; they also make fine pot plants, either indoors or out.

Cannas need a sunny, warm site protected against wind, and light, nutritious soil. Plant the rhizomes in pots or boxes in February or March under glass at a temperature of about 16°C (61°F); they should just barely be covered by the compost. In April pot on into 15—18 cm (6—7 in) pots. In May they can be planted in tubs or in the soil. During this period the plants should be fed and watered regularly. At the end of August stop watering so that the tubers can ripen well. In October, with the coming of the first frosts, cut the stems down to 10 cm (4 in), lift the tubers and allow them to partly dry. Store through the winter in damp, but *not* sodden, leaf-mould or peat at a temperature of 5—10°C (41—50°F).

The flowers of Indian shot (*Canna indica*).

55 Bulbs and Tubers: Small is Beautiful

One of the most delightful sights in the winter garden is the emergence of the snowdrops (*Galanthus*). First to show is the common snowdrop (*G. nivalis*), which brightens woodlands from January onwards, and may be from 7.5 cm (3 in) to 20 cm (5 in) tall. It has white, drooping flowers with greenish markings on the inner petals and flat, strap-like leaves. Its natural variety *G. n. reginae-olgae* flowers in autumn. The largest of the garden species, *G. elwesii,* is up to 25 cm (10 in) tall and flowers in February and March.

Almost as early is the yellow winter aconite (*Eranthis hyemalis*). Like the snowdrop, it likes to grow in rich soil under deciduous trees or shrubs. *Scilla tubergeniana,* one of the earlier bluebells, makes a delightful companion for snowdrops and winter aconite, as does the similar but darker-flowered *S. sibirica.* (The true English bluebell, which flowers in April-May, is classified as *Endymion nonscriptus.)* Also similar is the striped squill *Puschkinia scilloides* (sometimes listed as *Scilla sicula*), with its pale blue bell flowers which bloom in March—May.

Another delightful harbinger of spring is the *Crocus* (see the picture on the left). There are many species, but the two responsible for the largest number of easily available hybrids and cultivars are *C. chrysanthus* and *C. vernus,* the latter being the parent of the many large-flowered Dutch crocuses. The Dutch forms flower in March, while *C. chrysanthus* varieties are somewhat earlier.

The spring snowflake (*Leucojum vernum*) flowers in March and April. It has white campanulate flowers very similar to those of the snowdrop but more spherical in shape. Its cultivar *L. v.* 'Carpathicum' has a yellow edge to the tips of the flowers. The summer snowflake (*L. aestivum*), which blooms in April and May, is taller — up to 60 cm (2 ft) high — with somewhat larger flowers.

An unusual delight for the spring garden is the dog's tooth violet (*Erythronium denscanis*), with green purple- or brown-blotched leaves and, in April and May, lovely pinkish purple, six-petalled flowers. It has several cultivars. The American trout lily (*E. revolutum*) has a number of different forms, most with mottled flowers.

Grape-hyacinths (*Muscari*), mostly 20—25 cm (8—10 in) high, are attractive in borders, tubs and window boxes. *M. armeniacum* is particularly suitable for this purpose. There are many cultivars.

Autumn crocus (*Colchicum*) are particularly valuable plants for the garden because they flower from September to November. *C. autumnale,* 7.5—10 cm (3—4 in) tall, and the slightly larger *C. speciosum,* have many cultivars and hybrids in a wide range of colours. Colchicums have a different development cycle from most other bulbous and tuberous perennials. Their leaves grow at the beginning of April directly from the corm; they die in mid-June or early July. In September and October their flowers, like those of the related *Crocus,* grow directly from the corm. Seeds do not form until the following year. The entire plant is highly poisonous. Both *Crocus* and *Colchicum* look especially good if planted in drifts in rough grass; they are also suitable for the rock garden.

Many cyclamens are tender or half-hardy and are best treated as house plants, but *Cyclamen purpurascens,* syn. *C. europaeum,* which flowers in August and September, is completely hardy. Plant the corms just beneath the soil surface in August—September in a semi-shaded, sheltered site and in a rich, well-drained soil.

In places infested by voles, plant tubers and bulbs, particular those of crocuses and tulips, inside wire baskets.

The flowers of autumn crocus (*Colchicum*) brighten up the garden from September onwards.

56 Early Flowering Bulbs and Tubers

It is especially pleasing to have what are normally spring-flowering bulbs and tubers blooming in time for Christmas and the New Year. In the past the amateur gardener could achieve this only by using laborious and time-consuming 'forcing' techniques. Today, however, he can buy bulbs that have been specially prepared for early flowering and, moreover, have been treated to discourage disease and prevent premature rooting. Hyacinth, crocus, daffodil, scilla, chionodoxa, tulip and other specially treated bulbs are now generally available.

These bulbs need a well-balanced potting compost, such as John Innes No. 2 or bulb fibre, but they will not require early feeding because their preparation has induced the development of buds and immature flowers and foliage. Since the bulbs will be used as house plants, select attractive bowls or other containers rather than conventional garden pots. Line the bottom of the bowl with compost, and place the bulbs as close as possible to each other, filling the spaces in between with more compost. The tips of the largest bulbs — those of daffodils and hyacinths, for instance — should be above the compost surface; smaller bulbs should be covered completely.

You now need to encourage the bulbs to develop good strong roots and foliage. You do this by placing the containers in a cool, dark place. If you have to store them out of doors, cover them with a 15—20 cm (6—8 in) layer of peat or ashes which in turn should be covered with a sheet of black poly-

◀ A decoratively arranged bowl with forced tulips.

thene or other light-excluding material. You should examine the containers every two weeks to ensure that the compost is not drying out; water if necessary.

As soon as the leaf tips project 5 cm (2 in) above the compost, place the containers in the greenhouse or on a cool window sill in the house, maintaining a temperature of 10—12°C (50—54°F). When the leaves are 7.5—10 cm (3—4 in) long raise the temperature in gradual stages to about 18°C (64°F). If you want a succession of blooms, do not bring all the containers indoors at the same time. The plants will not be damaged if they are left out in the cold. By this means you can ensure that your favourite varieties bloom from mid-December to the end of March.

Hyacinths and some narcissi can be forced in water. Only the base of each bulb must be in the water.

When all the flowers in a bowl have died, place it in a light but cool place, maintaining a temperature of about 6°C (43°F) and keeping the compost moist. The bulbs can be planted out in the garden in April, making sure not to separate the roots from the compost.

Forcing tulips: (a) potted bulbs stored outside under layers of ashes and peat; (b) the bulbs should be planted close together in each pot; (c) bulbs may also be forced by placing a cone of thick black paper over the pot to exclude the light.

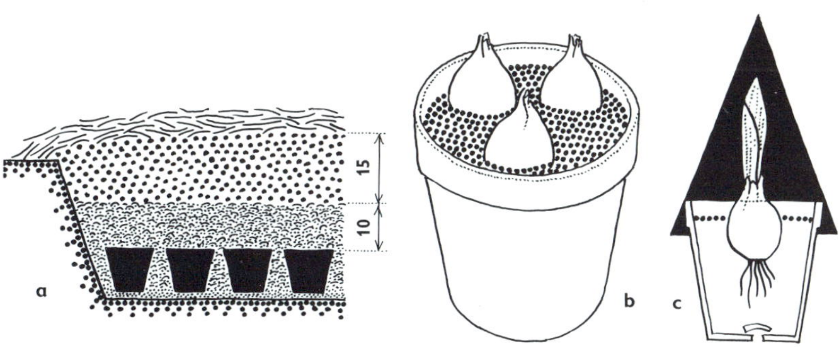

57 Annuals and Biennials: Their Role in the Garden

Many of our favourite flowering plants are annuals or biennials. Think of alyssums, snapdragons, begonias, marigolds, china asters, cornflowers, delphiniums, strawflowers, candytufts, sweet peas, mallows, toadflax, lobelias, tobacco plants, love-in-a-mist, phlox, salvias, nasturtiums, verbenas, violas — the list is almost endless. Then there are many tender or half-hardy perennials, such as petunias and sweet william, that are best treated as annuals.

●

Many of them make delightful cut flowers. As bedding plants, annuals and biennials can simply be used to create a riot of colour on their own, or they can fill in empty spaces between perennials and shrubs after spring-flowering plants have finished in beds, borders and rockeries. Each of the most popular annual species has a large number of cultivars, which further multiply the enormous range of colour, shape, texture and size at your disposal and which can be used in different arrangements in the garden every year. Biennials and most annuals can be easily grown from seeds, so the cost of producing quite a large area of stunning colour is relatively low.

◀ Use only the best-quality varieties of annuals for bedding. These examples are snapdragons (*Antirrhinum majus*).

When selecting individual groups of plants, first of all consider the character and size of the garden and of the individual beds and borders you intend to plant. Choose the less conspicuous varieties for the informally 'natural' environment of cottage gardens, while modern architecture seems to go best with the larger, more vividly coloured cultivars. In general, the most pleasing effects are achieved by mixing and blending varieties of different species to produce harmonious mixtures of colour, size and shape. Early-flowering species may be alternated with later ones to give a succession of colours throughout late spring and summer.

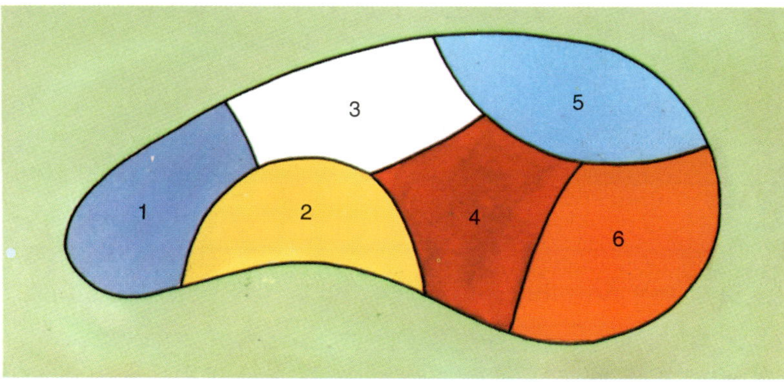

A more informal bed of annuals on a lawn: (1) floss flower (*Ageratum houstonianum*); (2) marigold (*Tagetes tenuifolia*); (3) *Chrysanthemum parthenium;* (4) snapdragon (*Antirrhinum majus* 'Nanum'); (5) Swan River daisy (*Brachycome iberidifolia*); (6) zinnia (*Zinnia angustifolia*).

A formal arrangement of bedding plants alongside a house wall: (1) sage (*Salvia splendens*); (2) African marigold (*Tagetes erecta*); (3) snapdragon (*Antirrhinum majus*); (4) petunia (*Petunia* x *hybrida*); (5) floss flower (*Ageratum houstonianum*).

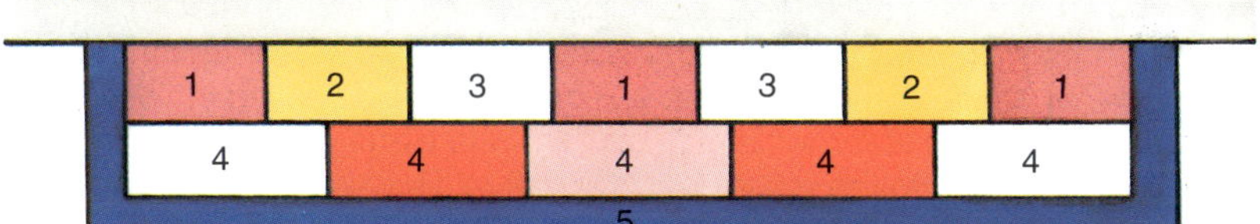

58 Siting Your Annuals and Biennials

Annuals and biennials grow best in a sunny and warm site. Semi-shaded sites are suitable only for some species, and in general shady sites must be avoided. Windy spots should also be avoided, especially for the taller varieties. Annuals and biennials like medium heavy, nutritious, well-drained soil. Heavy clay soil, which hardens on top after rain, is not suitable, particularly for annuals grown directly from seed: the soil crust makes it difficult for the seeds to germinate. (See Hint 2 for how to improve such soil.)

●

Do not feed the soil for annuals and biennials with manure or with organic or nitrogen-rich fertilizers. The plants would become too rampant in growth at the expense of their flowers and would be more vulnerable to fungal diseases. Most annuals do not even require composting, though the soil may benefit from this the autumn before planting. Some annuals will also do better if lime is raked into the soil the season before. Before sowing or planting, feed the soil with multi-element inorganic fertilizer.

◀ Butterfly flower (*Schizanthus* x *wisetonensis*) is an annual with orchid-like flowers.

Annuals can be grown on the same site for several consecutive years, with the exception of sweet pea (*Lathyrus odoratus*) and other species, such as pinks (*Dianthus*) and china aster (*Callistephus chinensis*), that are prone to fusarium wilt. Select a different bed for these plants every year to prevent a build-up of the fungi in the soil.

●

During the growing season water the plants according to their needs; the best time for this is early in the morning or in the evening. Avoid spilling water on the flowers. Cape marigold (*Dimorphotheca*), Livingstone daisy (*Dorotheanthus*), sea lavender (*Limonium sinuatum*), purslane (*Portulaca*), *Xeranthemum* and some others require drier soil. Grow these species in bare spaces over spring bulbs, which also require drier soil in the summer. By contrast, hollyhock (*Alcea*), love-lies-bleeding (*Amaranthus*), pot marigold (*Calendula*), *Cosmos,* love-in-a-mist (*Nigella*) and mignonette (*Reseda odorata*) require damper, though free-draining, soil.

China asters (*Callistephus chinensis*) need well-drained soil to prevent fusarium wilt.

Love-lies-bleeding (*Amaranthus caudatus*) can be used for mixed clump planting or as a low solitary plant.

59 Sowing Annuals Directly into Garden Soil

Species that are tolerant of spring frosts, or those which are sensitive to spring frosts but grow quickly, can be grown like this. Ideally, time your sowing of these species so that the plants do not sprout until after any May frosts.

●

Sow the seeds directly into well-worked soil. The planting distance depends on the species. In general, small seeds should be placed on the surface and barely covered with hand-sprinkled soil. Larger seeds are sown at a depth of 1—2 cm ($^1/_2$—1 in). Sow more sparsely into lighter soil than into heavier. Plants sown directly in the soil demand less water because their roots, which grow without interruption from germination, draw moisture from the deeper layers of soil.

●

From March to May sow hardy annuals such as pot marigold (*Calendula officinalis*), cornflower (*Centaurea cyanus*), *Chrysanthemum carinatum,*

◀ Pot marigold (*Calendula officinalis*) is suitable for group and spatial planting.

Plant *Centaurea imperialis* in mid-April directly on site.

Clarkia elegans, larkspurs (*Delphinium ajacis* and *D. consolida*), Californian poppy (*Eschscholtzia californica*), satin flower (*Godetia grandiflora*), candytuft (*Iberis umbellata*), summer cypress (*Kochia scoparia*), love-in-a-mist (*Nigella damascena*) and mignonette (*Reseda odorata*). Sow each of these annuals over a period of several weeks so that they will give you a succession of flowers.

●

More sensitive species like marigold (*Tagetes patula, T. tenuifolia*), larger nasturtiums (*Tropaeolum majus*) and the sun plant (*Portulaca grandiflora*) can be sown directly on warmer sites at the end of April, or a fortnight or so later if the weather is colder than usual.

●

Some annuals, such as *Delphinium,* can be sown in autumn, but most will need to be protected with cloches during the winter. Plants from such autumn-sown seeds are strong and flower earlier than spring-sown seeds.

●

If there is no available space in your beds and borders for direct sowing, raise the seedlings in a cold frame and plant them out once there is a free permanent site.

The decorative annual opium poppy (*Pappaver somniferum*) flowers in June and July with mostly full blossoms. It is sown directly on sites early in spring.

60 Starting Annuals under Glass

Those species with a longer development period and those killed by spring frosts need to be grown under glass as seedlings. Sow the seeds, usually in mid-March to mid-April, into a semi-warm frame or into bowls or boxes in a greenhouse or on a window-sill in a warm room. Some species must be pricked off (transplanted) into pots when the first couple of true leaves emerge; it is usually best to trim off a third of the roots first.

●

At the end of April or beginning of May harden off and plant the pre-grown seedlings of those species which tolerate lower temperatures in an outdoor bed. These species include *Dianthus chinensis, Iberis umbellata,* stock (*Matthiola incana*), *Limonium sinuatum, Penstemon hartwegii* hybrids, *Phlox drummondii,* rose-of-heaven (*Silene coeli-rosa*), and pink or red campion (*Silene pendula*). Species more sensitive to low temperatures should not be planted out until the end of May after the last frosts. These include china aster (*Callistephus chinensis*), *Chrysanthemum carinatum,* Livingstone daisy

The petunia (*Petunia*) is one of the longest-flowering annuals. It is a favourite component of beds, decorative pots, window boxes and hanging baskets.

(*Dorotheanthus bellidiformis*), blanket flower (*Gaillardia pulchella*), satin flower (*Godetia grandiflora*), *Helichrysum bracteatum* 'Monstrosum', large-flowered sun plant (*Portulaca grandiflora*), *Salpiglossis sinuata*, sweet scabious or pincushion flower (*Scabiosa atropurpurea*), all species of marigold (*Tagetes*), *Verbena* x *hybrida* and zinnias (*Zinnnia angustifolia* and *Z. elegans*).

Those annuals whose seedlings develop over a long period must be sown under glass as early as January or February. These include floss flower (*Ageratum houstonianum*), carnation or gilliflower (*Dianthus caryophyllus*), *Lobelia erinus*, petunia hybrids (*Petunia* x *hybrida*), *Salvia splendens*, and *Begonia semperflorens*. Sow the seeds into a John Innes or similar seed compost in bowls or boxes in a greenhouse or sunny room at a temperature of 18°C (64°F). When the seedlings show two true leaves, transplant them 4 cm (1 $^{1}/_{2}$ in) apart into boxes, and later into pots, in which they should be 10 cm (4 in) apart. Plant out the seedlings only when there is no further danger of frosts.

Sowing and pricking off annuals.

Zinnia (*Zinnia angustifolia* Haageana), with bicoloured flowers, is suitable for planting in clumps and also for cutting.

61 Growing Healthy Bedding Plants

The first requirement is to use only seed from a reputable supplier. And the second is to plant them at the correct time and in the site and soil best suited to the particular plants; these requirements may differ considerably from one variety of bedding plant to another.

During the growing season water the plants according to their particular needs, and after they have rooted feed them at the required intervals with multi-element fertilizer. Do not overfeed the seedlings as this encourages rampant leaf growth at the expanse of flowers. Hoe and weed the soil regularly. Remove flowers immediately they wilt; this will encourage the plants to grow further buds and extend the flowering season.

Plants showing evidence of established diseases, for example with spotted leaves, mildew, rust, etc., should be removed and burnt. Diseases can be prevented by well-balanced nutrition, especially by not over-feeding with nitrogen. Pull off the stricken leaves at the first sign of disease and spray the plants with a suitable fungicide. Deal with greenfly and other sucking insects if possible by picking them off the plants and destroying them; do nothing to discourage ladybirds and other insects that prey on aphids and other pests.

Salpiglossis sinuata bears its striking multicoloured, funnel-shaped flowers from midsummer to September. Several cultivars are available.

If plants are heavily infested, however, spray them with the appropriate insecticide.

In self-shedding species such as sweet pea (*Lathyrus odoratus*), stock (*Matthiola incana*), annual phlox (*Phlox drummondii*) and marigold (*Tagetes*), the best seeds can be removed for further growing. After drying out the fruits, remove and clean the seeds and store them in carefully labelled paper bags in a dry room. They usually take three or four years to germinate. Never pick seeds from F1 hybrids because plants grown from these seeds never come true to the characteristics of their parents.

Celosia argentea has two natural varieties: (a) *C.a. plumosa,* with pyramid-shaped flowers in red, yellow and pastel shades; and (b) cockscomb (*C.a. cristata*) with crested flower heads in red, orange or yellow. Both flower from July onwards and have numerous cultivars.

Seedling annuals, raised in pots in early and late spring, are useful for planting in any vacant spaces in beds and borders.

62 Popular Annuals for Cutting

The antirrhinum or snapdragon (*Antirrhinum majus*) has many cultivars differing in height and colour. The 'Maximum' group of cultivars are particularly suitable for cutting as they are 90—120 cm (3—4 ft) tall. By contrast, the semi-dwarf varieties of the 'Nanum' group are 45 cm (18 in) tall, while the 'Pumilum' group are no more than 15 cm (6 in) tall. Perhaps best of all for cutting are the 'Tetraploids' (also known as 'Tetra Snaps'), with superb colour spikes in a range of striking red, pink, orange, yellow and white single or double forms.

The China aster (*Callistephus chinensis*) has hundreds of cultivars with single and double flowers in a variety of forms in shades of red, pink, purple and white. Those strains most suitable for cutting include types with single, semi-double, double, pompon, ostrich-feather and quilled flowers. They vary in height from 30 to 75 cm (12—30 in) and in flowering season from July onwards until the first frosts. In addition, some of the dwarf strains, about 20—23 cm (8—9 in) tall, are ideal for growing in pots.

The fragrant carnation (*Dianthus carophyllus*) has both annual and biennial cultivars. Of the annual ones, the Chabaud strain is grown from seed sown in January or February; the seedlings are planted out in April and flower

◄ Sweet william (*Dianthus barbatus*) is a popular short-lived perennial.

throughout the summer. The biennial Grenadin strain is sown in May in a cold frame and planted out in August and September. The plants flower the following year from June to July.

The many varieties of satin flower (*Godetia grandiflora*) produce funnel-shaped flowers from July to August in single, semi-double and double forms. The cultivars vary in height from 30 to 38 cm (12—15 in) and the blooms may be red, pink, salmon-orange, crimson or white.

The garden hybrids of stock (*Matthiola incana*) produce fragrant spikes, up to 23 cm (9 in) long, of densely packed white, cream, yellow, pink, red or violet flowers in June and July.

Various forms of flowers of the China aster (*Callistephus chinensis*).

The *Zinnia* is popular for its decorative shape and colour. The most commonly grown is *Z. elegans,* whose cultivars, 60—75 cm (24 to 30 in) tall, have flowers measuring up to 7.5 cm (3 in) in diameter. The flowers, of various shapes, including dahlia-like forms, bloom from June until the autumn frosts. *Z. angustifolia* Haageana has somewhat smaller simple and full, single- or two-coloured flowers.

The snapdragon (*Antirrhinum majus*) is liked for its shape and the bright colours of its flowers.

63 Annuals for Formal Plantings

Among the most frequently used annuals for ornamental beds are the numerous hybrids of the fibrous-rooted *Begonia x semperflorens.* The 15 to 30 cm (6—10 in) high plants are covered from May to October in white, pink, red or pink-white flowers. The F1 hybrid cultivars have particularly rich flowers and are also better adapted to less sympathetic conditions. Seeds are sown under glass in February or March in shallow boxes filled with John Innes compost at a temperature of 15—16°C (59—61°F). The seedlings are pricked off into boxes when they show the first true leaf, and after hardening off can be planted out in May.

Pot marigold (*Calendula officinalis*) varieties make undemanding annuals that thrive even in poor conditions. They have yellow or orange single or double flowers. Most varieties are about 60 cm (2 ft) tall; there are also dwarf forms of about half that height. The seeds are sown directly into beds in March for summer flowers or in September for flowering in the following April or May. The taller varieties are also grown for cutting.

The treasure flower (*Gazania rigens*), a perennial usually grown as an annual, requires a sunny site to ensure that its white, yellow, pink, orange or brown-red flower-heads with distinctive centres can open up. It flowers from July until the autumn frosts. Plant out pot-grown seedlings at the end of May in beds with drier soil. The species is unsuitable for cutting because its flowers remain closed indoors.

Among the prettiest annuals are the garden varieties of petunia (*Petunia* x *hybrida*). They can be grown in decorative pots and in beds and borders. Varying from 20—38 cm (8—15 in) in height, they produce trumpet-shaped flower from June to October in various colours, including bicoloured forms. The seeds are sown under glass in March at 15—16°C (59—61°F) and the seedlings later pricked off into boxes. After hardening off in a cold frame, plant out in early June.

The fiery red terminal spikes of *Salvia splendens* (see the picture on the left) brighten the garden from June to October. Equally striking varieties with white, purple, salmon pink or scarlet flowers are also available. Raise seedlings from February-sown seeds. Transplant the small plants two or three times into successively bigger pots. Plant-out at the end of May into beds or decorative pots.

Marigolds (*Tagetes*) decorate garden beds with their long flowering from June until the autumn frosts. The French marigold (*T. patula*), which is rarely more than 30 cm (12 in) tall, is better for formal planting; the taller African marigold (*T. erecta*), with its large daisy-like flowers, is 60—90 cm (2—3 ft) tall and can be planted either formally or in clumps in a mixed border. It is also good for cutting. Both species have numerous garden varieties in yellow and orange.

Among the brightest of annuals are the *Verbena* x *hybrida* group of hybrids with their white, lilac, blue, pink or red flowers. The plants vary from 15—45 cm (6—18 in) in height and flower abundantly from June to September. Plant out at the end of May in sunny beds with good, fertile but not too damp soil.

The large-flowered African marigold (*Tagetes erecta*). This is one of the F_1 cultivars, 'Gold Lady'.

Petunia x *hybrida* F_1 variety 'Nora'.

64 Low-Growing Annuals for Summer Bedding

Choose plants that are not only decorative but have a long flowering season. The following compact favourites are ideal for the front of beds and borders as well as for containers of every kind.

The floss flower (*Ageratum houstonianum*), with its purple-blue flowers, goes well with many other annuals. The plants, 12—30 cm (5—12 in) tall, flower from June to the first autumn frosts. Raise the seedlings under glass at 16—18°C (61—64°F) in March and plant out, after hardening off, at the end of May.

The Livingstone daisy (*Dorotheanthus bellidiformis*) shows the beauty of its white, pink, crimson, orange or yellow flowers only on sunny days. It flowers from June to mid-August. Sow in March and April in a frame and plant out the seedlings at the end of May. The plants thrive only in well-drained soil.

The dwarf, spreading *Lobelia erinus* produces an abundance of tiny flowers from May well into autumn. There are many varieties, with blue, pink, or white flowers; mixed-colour strains are also available. They are raised from February-sown seeds and planted out at the end of May. Apart from the front of borders, this lobelia can be used in containers or as ground cover in rockeries.

Sweet alyssum (*Lobularia maritima*; sometimes listed as *Alyssum maritimum*) forms densely branched cushions with small white, lilac or violet flow-

◄ Nemesia versicolor.

ers from June to September. The species is rarely available, but there are many excellent varieties. They are sown in April directly into the site in pinches of seeds 25 cm (10 in) apart.

Among the most beautiful of border flowers is the large-flowered sun plant or purslane (*Portulaca grandiflora*), which is 15—23 cm (6—9 in) tall. It has single- or double-flowered varieties in various colours that bloom from June to the autumn frosts. It is a warmth-loving plant requiring a sunny site and well-drained soil. Sow under glass in boxes at the end of February and beginning of March. Plant out the seedlings at the end of May after they have been hardened off. The flowers open up only in full sunlight during the morning hours.

Nemesia versicolor flowers from June to August in various bright colours. Seedlings are raised under glass from seeds sown at the beginning of March and planted out in mid-May. Dead-head the wilted flowers to encourage further blooms.

Chrysanthemum parthenium, about 23—45 cm (9—15 in) high, flowers in July to September. Its numerous varieties have white or yellow flowerheads. Raise the seedlings from February-sown seeds and plant them out in mid-May. Hardy but short-lived perennials, the plants can be left in the bed after the flowers fade; after a mild winter they sometimes flower for a second season.

The Livingstone daisy (*Dorotheanthus bellediformis,* syn. *Mesembryanthemum criniflorum*), no more than 15 cm (6 in) high, makes a fine show at the front of a border.

The long-flowering floss flower (*Ageratum houstonianum*) is used for summer bedding and, in its taller forms, for cutting.

65 Annual Climbers

Morning glory (*Ipomoea purpurea*) is used most often for twining itself around fences, trellises, pergolas and arbours, and for covering walls up to 3 m (10 ft) in height. It has funnel-shaped, purple-fading-to-pink flowers, 9 cm (3 in) wide, arising from the leaf axils from July to the autumn frosts. Seedlings can also be raised in pots after April sowing, and planted out at the end of May in a suitable site. If they are not planted by a sunny wall or fence they should be grown on poles or pea-sticks. Dead-head the faded blooms to prolong the flowering period.

Maurandia species are tender or half-hardy climbing perennials usually used as half-hardy annuals and are grown in much the same way as morning glory. They reach about 4.5 m (15 ft) in height if grown under glass but not more than 2.1 m (7 ft) outdoors. Their purple, pink or white flowers bloom from May until late autumn. Sow the seeds under glass in February or March at a minimum 15°C (59°F) and prick out the seedlings into small pots when they are big enough to handle. Harden off before planting out in May. The two most easily available species are *M. barclaiana* and the similar but larger-flowered *M. erubescens*.

◄ Morning glory (*Ipomoea purpurea*) displays the beauty of its flowers only in the morning sun. It blooms from July to September.

Another twining annual which grows to a height of 6 m (20 ft) or more is cathedral bell, or cup-and-saucer plant (*Cobaea scandens*). From July to autumn it is decorated with blue-violet bell-shaped corollas within saucer-shaped calyces. Raise the seedlings under glass from seeds sown in February and March at 15°C (64°F). Harden off before planting out after the last frosts at the end of May. *C. scadens* is a hungry plant, but do not overfeed or it will grow foliage at the expense of flowers. It thrives in well-drained soil in a sunny, sheltered site; water frequently in dry weather. The plant's tendrils should be trained against a trellis, wire mesh or netting.

To create a beautifully scented wall in the garden, use one of the taller varieties of sweet pea (*Lathyrus odoratus*). Among the best are the Spencer group, up to 3 m (10 ft) high, which carry up to five fragrant flowers on each stem and range in colour from white through cream, lavender, mauve, pale blue, pink, to scarlet and ruby red. They bloom from June to September and need to be supported on canes or against a trellis or netting. Sow the seeds in March and April in good, well-drained, slightly alkaline soil. Prick out the tips of the young plants when they are no more than 10 cm (4 in) high to encourage the growth of lateral shoots.

Morning glory (*Ipomoea purpurea*) and scarlet runner bean (*Phaseolus coccineus*) are useful annuals for covering pergolas and other decorative structures.

66 Some Favourite Biennials

Among the most popular biennial plants suitable for bedding, for edging paths and for planting informally in rough grass are the many long-flowering hybrids of the garden pansy (*Viola* x *wittrockiana*). There are several groups of cultivars, differing in their time of flowering and size, number and colour of flowers. It is better to plant larger areas with single-coloured plants and use multi-coloured varieties in smaller clumps, in borders and in decorative pots. The seeds of winter-flowering types should be sown in July—August and planted in their flowering sites in September—October; they begin to flower in late autumn and continue until the following spring. Summer-flowering types are sown under glass in February—March and planted out in May; they will flower until September. The flowers of the cultivars may be red, yellow, blue, violet, white and bi-coloured.

The daisy (*Bellis perennis*) can be grown in the same way as the *Viola.* It has white, pink or red flower heads from April often until the beginning of October. Its flowers are suitable for cutting. Although it is a hardy perennial, it is more usually grown as an annual; the garden varieties have much larger and more colourful blooms than those of the common weed of lawns from which they derive.

The forget-me-not (*Myosotis sylvatica*) is a hardy biennial widely used in mixed borders and also for informal planting among trees. Sow the seeds in boxes in a cold frame or in seed beds in April—May. Prick out the seedlings into a nursery bed, grow them on, and plant them out in September. The small, fragrant sky-blue flowers bloom from April to June.

Some of the taller biennials are suitable for planting in clumps among other flowers. The Canterbury bell (*Campanula medium*) is highly decorative, with rich white, pink or dark violet flowers on stems 45—90 cm (15—36 in) high. The cup-and-saucer strain known as Calycanthema is particularly fine. Sow the seeds in March or April in a frame or greenhouse; prick off the seedlings, and plant them out at the end of August or beginning of September for flowering the following May to July.

The foxglove (*Digitalis purpurea*), with its purple, pink or white flower spikes up to 90 cm (3 ft) long, can also be grown in the same way. It prefers partial shade and must have soil that will not dry out in summer. There are many fine garden varieties that extend the colour range.

The scented wallflower (*Cheiranthus cheiri*), a shrubby perennial usually grown as a biennial, is a cottage garden favourite, flowering from April to June. It has many varieties, with flower colours in red, yellow, orange, scarlet, purple and crimson. Another old favourite is sweet william (*Dianthus barbatus*), whose densely packed bi-coloured flowers bloom from June to early August. As a solitary plant, the stately hollyhock (*Althaea rosea,* syn. *A. chinensis*) grows to a height of 2.5 m (9 ft) with, from July to September, single or double flowers up to 10 cm (4 in) across. There are many varieties, giving a choice of white, yellow, pink or red flowers. Raise seedlings from seeds sown in garden soil at the end of June and transplant to their flowering site in September or October.

A selection of garden pansies (*Viola* x *wittrockiana*).

Foxgloves (*Digitalis purpurea*) bloom in June and July.

67 Growing Plants for Dried Flowers

The best plants for this purpose bear flowers or fruits which retain their colours when dried.

The strawflower (*Helichrysum bracteatum*) is an annual widely used for dried bouquets. The plants are 90—120 cm (3—4 ft) high and bear white, yellow, brown or red flowers from July to October. For drying, cut off the flowers before they fully open. Tie them into bouquets and hang them upside down in a dark airy room. Sow strawflower seeds at the end of March or beginning or April in a frame; prick off the seedlings and plant them at the end of May in a sunny bed with light, well-drained soil.

The sunray (*Helipterum roseum*), which is rarely more than 38 cm (15 in) tall, is grown and used in a similar way. It has semi-double pink flowers in July and August. (Country-dwellers be warned: rabbits have a particular liking for these plants.)

Sea lavender (*Limonium sinuatum*) is 45 cm (18 in) high with decorative clusters of blue and cream flowers enclosed by green bracts in July to September. There are many garden varieties. Sow the seeds in March in a frame; plant out at the beginning of May. *L. suworowii* has small pink-red

Annuals suitable for dry bouquets: strawflower (*Helichrysum bracteatum*), sea lavender (*Limonium sinuatum*), *Helipterum roseum.*

flowers packed into a long spike that is up to 45 cm (18 in) long. It is widely used as a cut flower as well as for drying.

The stems of honesty (*Lunaria annua*), with their glossy silvery seed pods, make fine indoor decoration. The plant bears fragrant purple flowers in April to June. The seed pods follow soon after and should be cut no later than August.

●

Of the perennials used in winter bouquets, among the most popular are the yellow flowers of fernleaf yarrow (*Achillea filipendulina*); the steel-blue spherical flower of the globe thistle (*Echinops ritro*); the blue, prickly cone-shaped flowers of sea holly (*Eryngium alpinum*); the richly branched baby's breath (*Gypsophila paniculata*), with its cloud of tiny white or pink flowers; the mauve spikes of blazing star (*Liatris spicata*), up to 38 cm (15 in) long; the richly branched crowns of *Limonium tataricum,* with its small white flowers; and the bright orange lantern-shaped calyces, up to 5 cm (2 in) long, enclosing the fruit of the bladder cherry or Chinese lantern (*Physalis alkekengi*) in early autumn.

Of the bulbs used for dried bouquets, among the finest are the flowers of the alliums, of which the prettiest is *Allium albopilosum,* with its lilac-pink stars in June.

Of the annual grasses, the most suitable are switch grass (*Agrostis nebulosa*), barley (*Hordeum jubatum*), hare's-tail grass (*Lagurus ovatus*) and quaking grass (*Briza media*). Of the perennial grasses, the silvery pampas grass (*Cortaderia selloana*), porcupine grass (*Miscanthus sinensis*), feather grass (*Stipa pennata*) and feathertop (*Pennisetum alopecuroides*) have the most decorative inflorescences.

Dry bouquet made of various plant materials.

68 Container-Grown Plants

When selecting plants for growing in containers, consider first the size of the plants in relation to the size of the pots, vases, boxes, etc. in which they are to grow; and if the pots are decorative in their own right, make sure that their colours do not conflict with those of the plants you intend to grow in them.

●

Pelargoniums, often incorrectly termed geraniums, are widely used in every type of container, both indoor and outside. Zonal types (varieties of *Pelargonium* x *hortorum*), with interesting leaf markings, bear white, pink, red or orange flowers from May to October; ivy-leaved pelargoniums (*P. peltatum* varieties), with a more trailing habit, have ivy-shaped leaves (some edged in white or cream) and bear pink, lilac or white flowers throughout the summer. Petunias (*Petunia* x *hybrida*) available with white, cream, pink, purple, red, mauve, blue and various bi-coloured flowers, are also suitable for most types of container. Tuberous begonias (*B.* x *tuberhybrida*) and the vast range of fuchsia hybrids, most of which are hardy, are especially useful be-

◀ An attractive flower arrangement for the house.

cause they will grow happily in north- or east-facing sites as well as sunnier positions.

Large terracotta or other ceramic pots, boxes, troughs, etc., look especially good if used outdoors on patios, terraces, pathways and even strategically placed on lawns. Plant either one species in such containers or combine early and later flowering species to prolong their decorative season. Use some species with an erect habit of growth combined with others that droop over the side of the container. In the large containers think of having one dominating plant — a large, bright-flowered perennial, say, or even a shrub — and surround it with a variety of trailing plants, including some with unusually attractive foliage. Container-grown plants — and especially those in hanging baskets — require regular (and, in summer, frequent) watering and, at least until the end of summer, regular feeding with appropriate fertilizer. Make sure that all pots, boxes, etc., have drainage holes at the bottom.

●

There are scores of perennials and annuals of compact growth, and with interesting foliage as well as flowers, that are suitable for growing in containers of all kinds. These include alyssums and the related lobularias, *Anthemis,* wall cress (*Arabis*), pinks (*Dianthus plumaris* varieties), hellebores (*Helleborus*), which flower in winter, and polyanthus (*Primula* hybrids). Many of the smaller bulbous and tuberous plants also make excellent pot plants.

A portable decorative pot with stunted conifers as permanent occupants and annuals which can be changed every year.

Varicoloured primroses (*Primula*) are particularly suitable for decorative pots in spring.

69 Choosing a Site for a Rockery

While a rockery should be one of the dominant features in a garden, it should fit harmoniously into its surroundings; it should not be shaded by any structure or tree. The best foreground for a rockery is a well-kept lawn, and low evergreen bushes or another lawn provides a good background. The basic 'skeleton' of a rockery should consist of a small number of fairly large rocks or boulders. The spaces between the stones can be planted up with a rich variety of rock plants and alpines; and many attractive plants will colonize crevices or hollows in the rocks themselves.

●

In areas of average rainfall, the rockery should face either east or west: a south-facing slope may be prone to dry out in the summer; some rock plants may suffer from dehydration, although some others thrive in a dry environment. If your only option is a north-facing slope, your choice of plants will be narrower, although it will include quite a few shade-loving species and others that thrive at altitude.

A rockery is most effective for the colours of its plants in the spring.

Adjust a flat terrain before building the rockery. Dig an irregular hollow with slightly sloping sides and make a hillock of the dug up soil next to it. Waste construction material, hardcore and sand and gravel can be used to lay the foundation, thereby increasing the height of the hillock and creating good drainage — a prerequisite of a well-designed rockery. A pond can be constructed at the bottom of the slope. Keep things in proportion when planning the rockery. When completed and planted, it must not overhelm the rest of the garden by its size; nor, on the other hand, must it be so small that it looks like a hastily considered afterthought in the planning of the garden. Before any construction work, it is a good idea to make a series of sketches and plans of the garden as a whole, showing the area before and after construction of the rockery.

Adjusting the level of the terrain of a rockery: (a) correct way; (b) incorrect way.

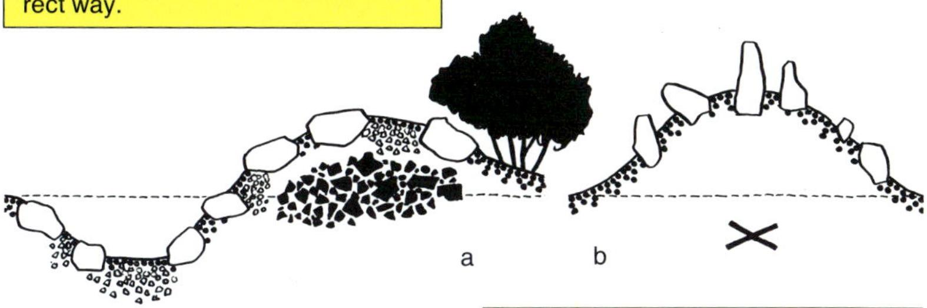

A rockery built against a garden wall may require construction of reinforcement in the shape of a buried inner wall to withstand the weight of the soil.

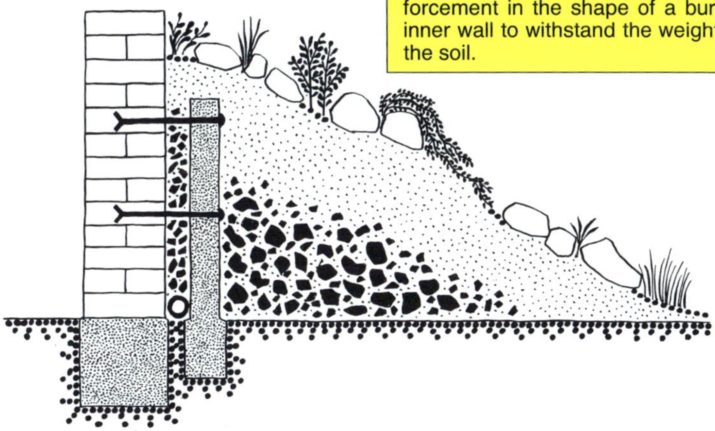

70 Choosing Your Stones

If a rockery is to look as natural as possible, it should use only one type of stone — if possible the dominant rock in the geology of your area. Nowadays you can order the stones directly from a quarry or from a firm of specialists.

●

You can specify the approximate size of stone and can get advice on the quantity required for your particular project. Local stone also has the likely advantage of being cheaper than an exotic one; and as transporting the stones is very expensive, buying from a local firm will almost certainly save you money.

●

Limestone and dolomite, which are both ideal for rockeries, should be grey or reddish in colour rather than completely white. Porous travertine, another type of limestone, is particularly suitable for rockeries planted with crevice-growing saxifrages and other plants.

The beauty of the rockery depends on the harmony created between the stones and the plants.

Many rocks, such as sandstone, are stratified; that is, they were originally formed by the deposition of strata, or layers, or rock-forming material. These rocks should always be laid with horizontal strata, but with the layers leaning gently back into the slope.

Avoid using artificial rocks made of concrete or reconstituted natural stones or natural rock that has been trimmed into a 'regular' shape. The aim is to imitate nature, and your rock garden should attempt to replicate small rock outcrops on an alpine slope.

Using stone slabs in construction of a rockery.

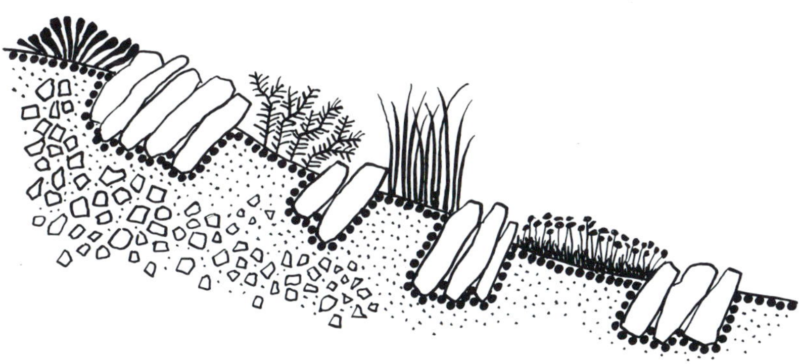

71 Constructing Your Rockery

Before building the rockery, remove all the underground stems and roots of perennial weeds from the soil. The most common way, but also the most laborious, is picking out even the smallest bits of roots manually when deeply hoeing the soil. Failing that, use a chemical weedkiller such as glyphosate, which is effective against couch grass and ground elder.

The soil in a rockery should be free-draining. So place at least a 20 cm (8 in) deep drainage layer of coarse waste material or gravel on heavy, clayey foundation soil, and then a layer, at least 25—35 cm (10—14 in) thick, of good top soil. If the soil is too heavy, mix in some peat, sand and/or gravel. For lime-loving plants, add some ground limestone and for heath plants fork in some pine-needle litter or a mixture of well-decomposed leaf mould and sand.

●

The best time for building a rockery is in autumn, so that the stones can settle in the ground by spring. Whether the slope of the site is gentle or steep, build from the base upwards. The steeper the slope, the closer will be one

◄ A rockery with a water spring.

layer of stones to the layer below it. If there are significant differences in the sizes of your stones, the larger ones should be in the lower layers. Start with the keystone — the stone from which all the others in the same course, or layer, radiate on either side. Dig out soil to accommodate the keystone to just below soil level. The base of the hole should slope slightly downwards towards the interior of the rockery. When the keystone is correctly placed, ram it into the slope so that it is absolutely firm. Now go through the same procedure with all the other stones in the lowest course. Although the size and shape of the stones in a course may vary, make sure that each stone is firmly against its neighbour. Failure to do this will result in soil spilling from the top to the bottom of the slope before all your plants have had time to establish themselves and cover the ground. Once the lowest course is firmly installed, the second and subsequent courses are added. As already mentioned, the steeper the slope, the closer will be each course to the ones above and below it. But whether they are close or relatively far apart, the base of each stone must be so positioned that it is below the level of the top of the stones in the course immediately below it.

If a lawn borders the bottom edge of the rockery, it is a good idea to cut the lawn back by about 60 cm (2 ft) and instal a gravel or paved path. This will not only improve access to the rockery; more importantly, it will help prevent an invasion of the rockery by grass and lawn weeds.

Thrift (*Armeria caespitosa*) is a mass of tiny flowers in spring.

The smaller bellflowers (*Campanula*) make delightful rockey plants.

72 When and How to Plant the Rockery

If, as suggested, you have built the rockery in the autumn, allow the stones and soil to settle down during the winter before beginning your planting programme in March and April. Potted seedlings can be planted out later.

The first thing to determine is the number of plants you need to buy. A rough rule of thumb is to assume that you will need one plant per 1—3 sq metres (1—3 sq yd), depending on the ultimate size and spread of each plant. You need to bear in mind that some of the plants will spread over the rock surface and tumble down towards the next level. The larger plants can be treated singly, as specimens; the smaller ones can be planted in groups. Take care not to swamp the smaller plants with the larger ones. It may seem, when you have completed your planting, that far too much bare soil and rocks is visible. Don't worry — within two or three years the plants will have begun to fill the empty spaces.

Individual species of rock plants often differ considerably in their demands on soil moisture, reaction to sunlight, and ability to withstand winter cold. It may therefore be necessary to divide the rockery into several sections, adjusting the soil conditions in each for, say, lime-loving plants and for those requiring acid soil.

Insert the plants in holes or in gaps. Cover the roots with soil, press down and water. For most common rock plants the ideal growing medium consists of 3 parts of garden earth, 3 parts of coarse sand and gravel, and 1 or 2 parts of peat. Water the plants in the evening or early morning. Watering during a warm day is not good for the plants. For the first few days after planting, it is a good idea to shade the plants with clay flower-pots to encourage root development.

Which plants are the most suitable for rockeries? For sunny sites the choice is enormous but might include *Aethionema* x 'Warley Rose', gold dust (*Alyssum saxatile*), *Androsace alpina, Anemone blanda, Aquilegia bertolonii* and *A. flabellata, Armeria maritima, Aubrieta* hybrids, *Campanula carpatica, Chionodoxa luciliae, Colchicum speciosum, Cotoneaster microphyllus, Crocus chrysanthus* hybrids, *Cytisus ardoinii, Daphne alpinum, Eranthis hyemalis, Erica carnea* 'Springwood White', *Erigeron aureus, Eryngium alpinum, Genista pilosa, Geranium cinereum* and *G. sanguineum, Hebe pagei, Helianthemum* 'Wisley Primrose', *Helichrysum frigidum, Iberis compacta, Juniperus communis* cultivars, *Leucojum autumnale, Lewisia* hybrids, *Linum flavum, Narcissus cyclamineus, Nerine bowdenii, Phlox douglasii* 'May Snow' and 'Rosea', *Picea abies* 'Gregoriana', *Pinus mugo* 'Mops', *Potentilla aurea, Primula auricula* hybrids, dwarf *Rhododendron, Saxifraga* x *apiculata, S. fortunei, S.* 'Tumbling Waters', *Scilla sibirica, Sempervivum arachnoideum, Sisyrinchium bermudianum, Soldanella alpina, Spiraea* x bumalda 'Nyewood', *Thymus lanuginosus, Tiarella wherryi, Trollius acaulis, Veronica gentianoides, Viola* 'Haslemere', *Zauschneria cana.*

Shade lovers include *Adiantum pedatum, Arenaria balearica, Asarina procumbens, Cornus canadensis, Cyclamen cilicium* and *C. coum, Erythronium dens-canis, Galanthus nivalis, Gaultheria cuneata, Haberlea rhodopensis, Hepatica nobilis, Nomocharis mairei, Polygonum vaccinifolium, Primula juliae, Ramonda myconi, Sarcococca hookeriana humilis, Saxifraga* 'Winston Churchill'.

Saxifrages (*Saxifraga*) of the *Euaizoonia* section thrive in natural or specially created rock crevices.

73 Looking after Your Rockery

Remove weeds, even in their youngest stage of growth, from the rockery throughout the year. Use herbicides such as glyphosphate, which attacks weeds through their foliage, does not affect the soil, and is effective against perennial weeds as well as annuals.

●

During the growing season rock plants require plenty of moisture, particularly those on south-facing slopes. In order to ease this work, an irrigation system can be built in during construction of the rockery.

●

If you do not have such a system, apply water with a watering-can or hose fitted with a fine sprinkler attachment. Water carefully so that the plant are not damaged and the soil is not washed away down the slope. Avoid watering the rockery at mid-day when the stones are hot.

◀ A rockery with small flowering plants.

Protect evergreen rock plants against the cold with a light cover of conifer branches, so that the sun does not damage them during a period of hard frost. In spring, as soon as there is no more danger of frost, gradually remove the cover, the best time being during overcast weather. In regions with mild winters a cover is not necessary. Cover plants which do not tolerate damp during the resting period (e.g. *Lewisia*) in the autumn with a cloche and remove it in the spring.

●

In spring cut back all herbaceous material that died down the previous autumn. Improve the soil in shady areas with a mulch of leaf mould or well-rotted garden compost. The whole area should also be given an annual feed of bonemeal.

The wick method of applying Roundup herbicide to foliage is ideal for destroying stubborn perennial weeds.

Irrigation of rockeries: (a) by underground piping, (b) by sprinkler.

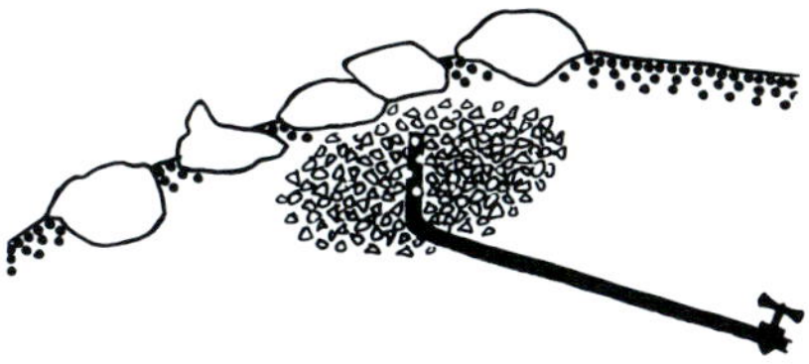

a

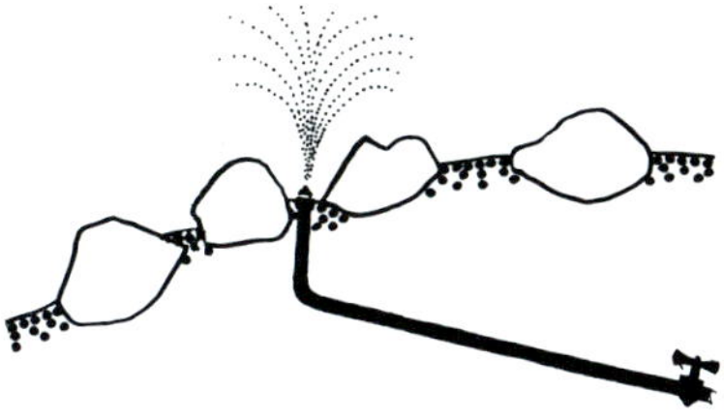

b

74 Propagating Rock Plants

The easiest way to propagate rock plants is by vegetative methods, which ensure that they retain the original qualities of their parent plants. The usual way is to divide the crowns in spring or at the end of summer. In summer propagation, trim the surface part of the plant in proportion to the roots so that the divided part can take root easily. In certain species, such as *Androsace, Viola odorata* and *Phlox subulata,* leave the offshoot to root.

●

In July and August propagate mature summer growers such as *Aubrieta, Achillea tomentosa,* rock rose (*Helianthemum*), *Dianthus, Saxifraga,* speedwell (*Veronica*) and stonecrops (*Sedum*). For cuttings use 2—3 long stolon cymes which have had their buds and flowers removed. Encourage rooting with the use of hormone rooting powder. Plant the cuttings in boxes or pots, placing the pots into sand in a frame. Keep the growing medium adequately moist.

◄ *Alyssum repens* is propagated from seeds or by division.

Propagate low-growing daphnes (*Daphne*), heaths (*Erica*), heathers (*Calluna*), etc. in the spring by layering — that is, by burying a ground-level branch into the soil and securing it with a hook or peg. Water well and keep the soil moist in dry periods. In the autumn, sever the layered stem from the parent plant.

●

Plant species, as distinct from hybrids and cultivars, can be propagated from their seeds; seedlings are generally more resilient than plants propagated vegetatively. Most seeds can be sown in spring, but those of species such as *Adonis,* winter aconite (*Eranthis*), *Pulsatilla* and others must be sown immediately after ripening in the autumn. Sow seeds into bowls or pots filled with John Innes or equivalent seed compost. Sow the seeds sparsely on the surface, cover them with a thin layer of compost, and water carefully. Bury the pots to their rims in sand in a cold frame. When the seedlings have developed two or three true leaves, prick them off into small pots. Do not plant them in a permanent bed until the following year.

We can collect seeds of the rock plants in our own rockery or in the country. The ripe fruits are left to dry in open containers for several days. Then the seeds are shaken out or rubbed out, sieved and put into small paper sachets until the sowing time.

Eriogonum umbellatum is a wonderfully flowering semi-bush rockery plant. It can be propagated by division or from cuttings.

75 Dry-Stone Walls

If the terrain in your garden is hilly, you can make it easier for gardening by converting the slope into terraces supported by dry-stone walls. The terraces can be 1 m (3 $^{1}/_{4}$ ft) or more from front to back.

●

As in rock-garden construction, use a single type of natural stone. If the dry wall joins on to a building with a stone base wall, it should obviously be built from the same type of stone.

●

Build the wall as follows: First, dig a hole for the concrete foundation. This should be 20—40 cm (8—16 in) deep, depending on the height of the wall, with its surface 10 cm (4 in) below the surface of the soil. For the wall, use square rather than rounded stones so that the soil holds well in the gaps. Place the stones in courses, making sure they bind well together to produce

◄ An extensive rockery ending in a dry stone wall.

A rockery with dry walls.

a firm structure. If the stones vary in size, use the bigger ones in the bottom courses and the smaller ones in the top courses. The wall should lean slightly into the terrace; each course should be about 3—4 cm (1—1 $^1/_2$ in) further towards the terrace than the one below it. As you complete each course, cover it with a layer of good, slightly moist garden soil, filling in the gaps between the stones; as you do this, first fill any large gaps with smaller stones.

●

While constructing the wall, insert rock plants into the earth in the gaps. To create bigger areas of plants, plant one species in several neighbouring gaps. Cover the seedling roots with good moist garden soil mixed with sand and peat.

●

Make sure that the terrace area against the wall has good, well-drained soil. The plants growing in the wall will take root in this soil.

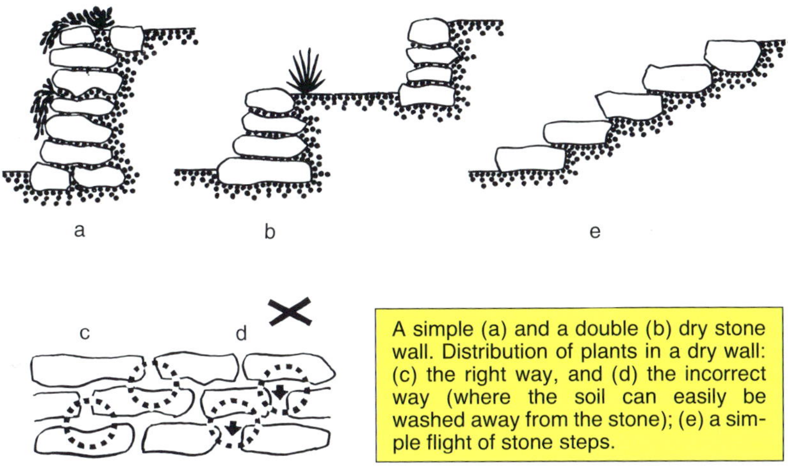

A simple (a) and a double (b) dry stone wall. Distribution of plants in a dry wall: (c) the right way, and (d) the incorrect way (where the soil can easily be washed away from the stone); (e) a simple flight of stone steps.

76 The Best Plants for Dry Walls

Virtually all rock plants are suitable which will grow in the gaps. The best are species which do not require much care.

●

Combine plants in such a way that the dry wall is in flower for as long as possible. Plant warmth-loving and dry-loving species on the sunny side.

Early spring-flowering plants are yellow *Alyssum,* white wall cress (*Arabis*), lilac, blue Pulsatilla, pink, red, blue or violet *Aubrieta,* candytuft (*Iberis*) and various species of saxifrages (*Saxifraga*), which are diverse in colour and shape of flowers.

In mid-spring dry walls are decorated with pink and red carnations (*Dianthus*), alpine aster (*Aster alpinus*), whose pink, white or blue flowers have a yellow centre, the white or pink baby's breath (*Gypsophila repens*), *Phlox subulata,* etc.

◄ In a formal garden, especially in places with a high level of underground water, a rockery can be built on a raised bed constructed, as here, from stone slabs or from such materials as old railway sleepers.

In summer there are blue bellflowers (*Campanula cochlearia, C. poscharskyana,* etc.), red, pink or white wild thyme (*Thymus praecox* ssp. *arcticus*), pink soapwort (*Saponaria ocymoides*), various coloured stonecrops (*Sedum*) and houseleeks (*Sempervivum*), trailing blue *Nepeta nervosa,* and creeping speedwell (*Veronica repens*) with small blue, pink or white flowers.

●

On walls facing away from the sun, where there is more moisture, grow thrift (*Armeria caespitosa*) whose small needle-like leaves are covered with numerous little pink flowers. Violet-flowering *Haberlea,* blue *Ramonda,* yellow *Corydalis,* white and pink flowering miniature rock jasmines (*Androsace*), and saxifrages that tolerate shade (*Saxifraga umbrosa, S. caespitosa*) are also suitable.

●

Plants demanding more moisture should be planted in the bottom part of the wall and dry-loving ones towards the top. Dwarf shrubs and low-growing bulbous plants can be grown on top of the wall. Protect evergreen plants in winter, particularly those exposed to full sunlight.

Steps in a low dry-stone wall.

77 Building a Mini-Rockery

A large rockery and extensive dry-wall terracing can be expensive in time, materials cost, and physical effort. But a rockery can be as small as you like, and in small city gardens your only option may be an inexpensive mini-rockery.

•

The first thing you need is a suitable vessel. The ideal container is one of those old-fashioned stone or ceramic kitchen sinks or troughs. It must be at leat 25 cm (10 in) deep and have an adequate drainage outlet either at the bottom or on the side. If you cannot get hold of one of these, you will find that many of the larger garden centres sell large concrete troughs for this purpose.

•

The best site for the mini-rockery is a regularly mown lawn, a terrace or patio, or the balcony of a house or flat. Place the vessel on some sort of base, the best being flat stones.

Plant only the smallest species of alpines in a mini-rockery in a stone trough.

Place a drainage layer of pebbles in the bottom quarter of the vessel, cover it with a plastic netting to act as a filter, and fill the trough with light but rich soil. Embed stones into the surface of the soil; the best are of porous travertine. Grow small rock plants in the mini-rockery such as miniature rock jasmines (*Androsace*), *Arenaria,* sea pink (*Armeria caespitosa*), *Edraianthus pumilio,* spring gentian (*Gentiana verna*), small, compact, drooping *Phlox subulata,* moss campion (*Silene acaulis*), etc. Of the woody plants, the best are the most dwarf cultivars of conifers and deciduous plants. The bigger ones are planted at the edge of the vessel so they can trail over the side. Cover the soil surface between the plants with fine gravel.

●

During the growing season the mini-rockery plants should be watered according to need, but take care not to over-water. In spring the plants should be fed occasionally with multi-element fertilizer.

A ceramic trough with rock plants: (a) drainage layer; (b) drainage filter; (c) soil (a mixture of equal parts of garden soil, pine needle litter and coarse sand or fine gravel).

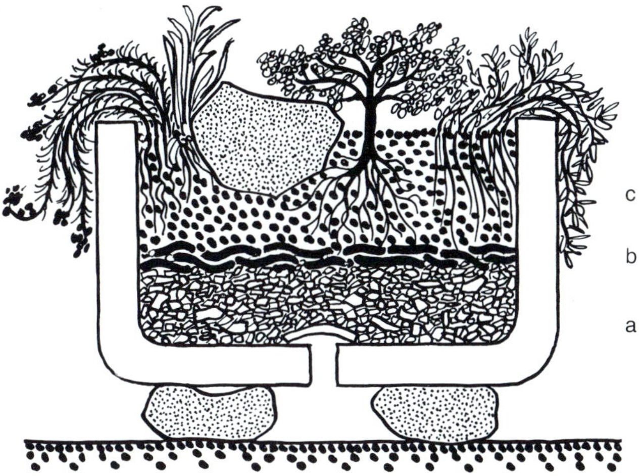

78 Rockery Plants: Early Spring

Some of the saxifrages (*Saxifraga*), notably *S.* x *apiculata* (yellow flowers), *S. burserana* (white), *S.* x 'Cranbourne' (pink), *S. haagii* (yellow), *S. irvingii* (pink), *S.* x 'Riverslea' (purple red), are among the earliest-flowering rock plants. They form small hummocks with short-stemmed or stemless flowers. Most are 5—10 cm (2—4 in) high with a spread of 30—45 cm (12—18 in). In spring they require plenty of moisture. The more sensitive species should be covered in winter with cloches, and the site must be free-draining so that the plants do not suffer from boggy soil; mix in grit to help drainage. Saxifrages need a limy soil, and most of them do better in a semi-shaded site.

The large-flowered *Pulsatilla grandis* has beautiful violet campanulate flowers with numerous yellow stamens; some cultivars have white or red flowers. The plants are decorative even after wilting, with their balls of furry seeds. A somewhat earlier cultivar is the particularly beautiful *P. slavica,* which has lighter violet flowers 8 cm (3 in) in size. The leaves grow after the flowers have wilted and are more roughly divided than those of *P. grandis.* Pulsatillas like a sunny, warm position in well-drained, humus-rich soil. A good companion for it is *Adonis* with its large golden yellow flowers. *A. amurensis* 'Flore-pleno', with its more roughly divided leaves, flowers in Feb-

◄ Saxifrages (*Saxifraga*) of the *Euaizoonia* section.

ruary—March, and *A. vernalis,* with its finely dissected leaves, flowers a month later.

Whitlow grass (*Draba aizoides*) grows well in the cracks between the stones. It makes little leafy hillocks of stiff, linear leaves, with small yellow flowers in April. It thrives on a sunny and rather dry site with good drainage.

Candytuft (*Iberis saxatilis*) is suitable for small rockeries; it is rarely more than 7.5 cm (3 in) high. It creates evergreen bushes with a lot of white flat-topped flowerheads. *I. sempervirens* 'Little Gem', also with white flowers, is slightly larger. After the flowers wilt, cut off about a third or half of the plant.

Blue-eyed mary (*Omphalodes verna*), one of the perennial navelworts, with its delicate flowers, resembles the true forget-me-not and flowers from February to May. It is about 15 cm (6 in) high and about twice as wide and grows best on a semi-shaded site with humus-rich, slightly limy, well-drained soil. (The somewhat similar *O. luciliae* is, however, a sun-lover and flowers throughout the summer.)

The richly white-flowered wall cress (*Arabis caucasica*), with its cushion-like and somewhat invasive habit, is suitable for larger rockeries. Its less invasive variety *A.c.* 'Flore-pleno' is better for smaller areas. Both prefer partial shade and well-drained soil, and both enjoy a long flowering season from February until June.

Early in the spring low-growing perennials, such as those described in Hint 19, and small bulbs, as in Hint 55, can also be grown in a rockery.

Pulsatilla (*Pulsatilla grandis*) is a typical spring-flowering rock plant of warmer regions.

The spring adonis (*Adonis vernalis*) has also been cultivated from full-flowered forms.

79 Rockery Plants: Mid-Spring

Among the most beautiful rock plants are the garden varieties derived from *Aubrieta deltoidea,* a hardy evergreen. The mat-forming plants, 8—10 cm (3—4 in) high, with heavy, toothed leaves, flower from April to June, depending on the cultivar, with blue, violet, pink and red single or double flowers; in some varieties, the leaves are edged in white or gold. Aubrietas thrive on sunny and warm sites in fertile, well-drained, limy soil.

Good companions for the aubrietas are the undemanding golden-yellow-flowering varieties of *Alyssum saxatile.* The 25 cm (10 in) high clusters with grey-green, furry leaves flower in April. The similar *Alyssum montanum* is smaller, less furry and also has yellow flowers. Alyssums are particularly suitable for growing between stones, on top of rockeries, and in crevices in dry walls.

●

Another group of attractive spring rock plants are the varieties of moss phlox (*Phlox subulata*), up to 10 cm (4 in) high and producing red, pink, purple, white and lilac blue flowers in April and May. In recent years varieties of more

◄ *Aubrieta, Arabis* and moss phlox (*Phlox subulata*) are among the most beautiful of the spring-flowering cushion-like rock plants.

compact growth, suitable especially for small rockeries, have become available. Protect moss phloxes in winter with a cover of conifer branches. Phlox grows best on sunny sites with good humus-rich, free-draining soil.

Miniature rock jasmines (*Androsace*) are especially good for smaller rockeries and dry walls. These delicate but hardy perennials with their decorative, tufted rosettes of leaves, have white, pink, red or yellow flowers composed into umbels. They tolerate sunny or semi-shaded sites with well-drained soil. Mid-spring species include *A. helvetica* and *A. primuloides.*

Thrifts (*Armeria*) form lovely evergreen cushions in the rockery. The lowest-growing is *A. caespitosa,* 5—7.5 cm (2—3 in) high, which is covered in April and May with a mass of pink flowers. It likes ordinary, preferably well-drained soil in full sun. The taller *A. maritima* is 15—30 cm (6—12 in) high and produces pink flowers early in May. There are several good varieties producing white, pink or rose-red blooms.

Among the most popular spring rock plants are the gentians, notably varieties of *Gentiana acaulis* (syn. *G. clusii*). They are only 5—10 cm (2—4 in) high, have erect trumpet-shaped flowers of a beautiful deep blue and they grow well in a sunny site with good, adequately damp, lime-free soil. *G. verna,* of a similar size, flowers in May; it likes a soil containing lime.

Among the most popular rock plants is the trumpet gentian (*Gentiana acaulis,* syn. *G. clusii*), which flowers in May and June.

A spring rockery with lewisias. The soil is covered with rubble.

80 Rockery Plants: Early Summer

True gems in the rockery at the beginning of the summer are the lewisias (*Lewisia cotyledon*) and their varieties. Between 15 and 30 cm (6—12 in) high, they bear panicles of pink, salmon pink, apricot or orange flowers, with dark or light stripes, from a ground rosette of tough evergreen leaves, in May and June. Lewisias need partial shade and rich, well-drained soil containing plenty of gravel. The tops of the roots must be protected against excessive wet in winter, preferably with a generous layer of chippings. In the autumn cover the plants with a cloche or sheet of glass to keep them dry through the winter.

●

At the beginning of the summer, clove pinks (*Dianthus caryophyllus*) have white, pink or red flowers with entire or frizzy edged flowers. They do not tolerate soil that is too wet.

The numerous varieties of rock rose (*Helianthemum nummularium*) bear white, yellow, orange, pink or red single or double flowers in June and July.

◄ Lewisia (*Lewisia cotyledon*) is one of the prettiest rock plants imported from the western United States.

Dead-heading induces a second period of flowering from August into mid-autumn. The single flowers usually last only for one day, but further ones open up immediately. The double flowers last longer. Plant rock roses on a sunny site in light, limy soil.

Edelweiss (*Leontopodium alpinum*), which is only 20 cm (8 in) high, is the symbol of mountains in a rockery. Its inflorescence is composed of several whitish flowerheads around which are woolly white bracts. It flowers eagerly on a sunny site in June and July in slightly damp, well-drained, sandy soil. It grows best in rockery crevices.

Soapwort (*Saponaria ocymoides*) is a cushion-like rock plant which bears abundant rose-pink flowers from July. It is not a demanding plant as to its environment or care. It likes light, limy soil. After wilting cut the plant down and cover it for the winter to protect against damp. Two excellent varieties are *S.o.* 'Compacta' and 'Rubra Compacta'.

Oenothera missouriensis is an excellent perennial for rockeries as well as borders. It is 10—15 cm (4—6 in) high, its main stems usually recumbent. Its brilliant yellow flowers, up to 7.5 cm (3 in) wide, open from June onwards in the evenings.

Finally, the purple-flowered species of *Edraianthus,* closely related to *Campanula,* open their bell-like flowers in June. They associate well with golden flax (*Linum flavum*), with its yellow flowers, and the sky-blue flowers of *L. perenne.*

Edelweiss (*Leontopodium alpinum*).

The full-flowered rock rose (*Helianthemum nummularium*).

81 Rockery Plants: Mid-Summer

In this season the rockery becomes the domain of perennial bellflowers (*Campanula*). Most have blue, purple, cream or white flowers. They thrive on a sunny and semi-shaded site with porous, medium-heavy, humus-rich soil. Among the most popular species is the 10—25 cm (4—10 in) high Carpathian harebell (*C. carpatica*) with wide campanulate flowers. It has several excellent cultivars. Two good dwarf campanulas, not more than 10 cm (4 in) high, are *C. arvatica* and *C. aucheri.*

Achillea tomentosa, a dwarf yarrow, with golden yellow flower-heads and feathery silver-green leaves, likes light and dry soil on a sunny site.

Summer favourites include the crane's-bills (*Geranium*), with lovely shaped leaves and bowl-shaped flowers. They grow well in poorer soil (if the soil is too rich it affects the flower production). Sprinkle limestone rubble around the plants and protect them in winter against wet weather. *G. cinereum,* 10—15 cm (4—6 in), and its many varieties, with pink to red flowers with dark veins or an eye in the centre, are among the most popular crane's-bills for the rockery; others are *G. dalmaticum* and *G. pylzowianum,* the latter an excellent ground-cover plant.

◀ Carpathian harebell (*Campanula carpatica*).

Of the gentians flowering in summer, the variety most often grown is the 15—20 cm (6—8 in) high *Gentiana septemfida lagodechiana* with its light blue flowers growing in clusters on drooping herbaceous stems. It likes sunny and semi-shaded sites with free-draining, humus-rich soil. The 40 to 50 cm (16—24 in) high willow gentian (*Gentiana asclepiadea*) is suitable for a damp, partly shaded corner of a larger rockery. Its dark blue flowers grow in the axil of the leaves along the entire length of the herbaceous stems.

An altogether undemanding plant for adequately damp soil is the long-flowering self-heal (*Prunella grandiflora*), whose varieties have violet, pink or white flowers on 15 cm (6 in) stems. Self-heal is invasive, so dead-head the plants throughout the summer to prevent them self-sowing.

Wild thyme (*Thymus praecox* ssp. *arcticus*) forms a low, thick mat of foliage with pink, red or white flowers, and is a must for sunny sites with sandy, porous soil. It lasts for years without any care. Use it, for example, for covering bare patches after spring bulbs finish.

Common marjoram (*Origanum vulgare*) is 30—45 cm (12—18 in) high and develops dense panicles of tiny rose-purple flowers in July and August. The plant is a widely used culinary herb and has a pleasant scent. *O.v.* 'Aureum' has golden yellow leaves when young.

The altogether undemanding stonecrops (*Sedum*) are grown in bigger spaces with porous, rather less fertile soil on a sunny or semi-shaded site. The varieties of *S. spurium,* with pink, red and white flowers, and orange stonecrop (*S. kamtschaticum*) with orange-yellow flowers, both bloom in midsummer.

In order to brighten up the rockery, at the end of May plant some low-growing annuals which flower in midsummer and later. Particularly suitable are the mesembryanthemums (*Dorotheanthus*), *Lobelia, Nemesia strumosa* varieties, cape marigold (*Dimorphotheca annua*) and *Ageratum houstonianum.*

A summer rockery is made beautiful by the Livingstone daisy (*Dorotheanthus bellidiformis*).

82 Rockery Plants: Autumn Colour

Far fewer perennial rock plants flower in the autumn than in summer. But, if you plan with care, your rockery will still offer interesting colour even at this time of year. Among the most beautiful of all rock plants is the autumn gentian, *Gentiana sino-ornata.* The superb blue flowers, which have darker blue and greenish-yellow stripes, are 5 cm (2 in) long and bloom from September to November. This plant requires free-draining but moist, humus-rich, lime-free soil, a semi-shaded site and protection in the winter.

The campion (*Silene schafta*) forms 10—15 cm (4—6 in) high drooping sprays of pink to carmine red flowers from July through to October. It thrives best on a sunny site in light, limy soil.

Chrysanthemum weyrichii is 10—15 cm (4—6 in) high and bears 5 cm (2 in) wide flowers with pink ray florets and yellow discs from late September. It requires well-drained, gritty soil in full sun.

Germander (*Teucrium chamaedrys*), a hardy sub-shrub, forms spikes of pink-purple flowers from July and into September. It requires a warm site with drier soil containing plenty of calcium.

◀ Various species of evergreen succulent houseleeks (*Sempervivum*) decorate the rockery with their leafy rosettes throughout the year.

Houseleeks (*Sempervivum*), with their rosettes of tough, fleshy leaves, provide a decorative effect in a rockery. The individual species differ in the size, shape and colour of the leafy rosettes. The rosettes tend to come in various shade of green, brown, red and violet, sometimes with differently coloured tips. During the growing season, mainly in July, the mature rosettes form 10—20 cm (4—8 in) high stems with flowers. When the flowers wilt, remove the old rosettes. Of the numerous hardy species, cobweb houseleek (*S. arachnoideum*) is very charming with its small rosettes covered in silvery cobweb-like hairs. Houseleeks grow best on a sunny and dry site with limy soil. Only *S. arachnoideum* does not tolerate lime. The best position for houseleeks is between stones. However, even a little soil in the hollow of a stone is enough for a houseleek to root and grow well. Species with small rosettes are best planted in mini-rockeries.

Of the tuberous plants, those that brighten up a rockery in the autumn are such species as *Cyclamen purpurascens,* autumn crocuses (*Colchicum*), and the few autumn-flowering *Crocus* species (*C. banaticus, C. kotschyanus, C. niveus,* and *C. speciosus*).

Of the annuals still flowering in this season, there are the sun plant (*Portulaca grandiflora*), marigold (*Tagetes tenuifolia*), some garden varieties of *Lobelia erinus,* etc.

The cyclamen (*Cyclamen purpurascens*) requires a semi-shaded site with humid and limy soil.

The marigold (*Tagetes tenuifolia*) flowers from July until the first autumn frosts.

83 Woody Plants for the Rockery

Dwarf forms of some trees and many small shrubs make excellent plants for the larger rockery. It is vital, however, to check on the size of the mature specimen before buying a woody plant, otherwise it many have to be removed after only a few years.

Today many garden centres as well as specialist suppliers offer dwarf forms of a wide range of the most popular conifers. Some of these cultivars are simply miniature versions of the parent species; others have been specially developed to have a low, spreading habit. You can also help to further restrict the final size of some trees by trimming back young growths at particular times of the year.

●

Among popular conifers, many excellent dwarf forms include the following: silver fir *Abies balsamea* 'Hudsonia', about 90 cm (3 ft) high on maturity; cypresses *Chamaecyparis lawsoniana* 'Minima' and 'Nana', 90—120 cm (3—4 ft), *C. obtusa* 'Kosteri', 90 cm (3 ft), and *C. pisifera* 'Compacta', 60 cm

◀ Using conifers in a rockery.

(2 ft), and 'Plumosa Pygmaea', 90 cm (3 ft); junipers *Juniperus chinensis* 'Pfitzerana', 90 cm (3 ft), *J. communis* 'Compressa', 60 cm (2 ft), and *J. squamata* 'Blue Star', 30 cm (1 ft); Norway spruce *Picea abies* 'Nidiformis', 30 cm (1 ft), and Canadian spruce *P. glauca* 'Nana', 90 cm (3 ft); mountain pine *Pinus mugo* 'Mops', 35 cm (14 in); white cedar *Thuja occidentalis* 'Rheingold', 90 cm (3 ft), and 'Dumosa', 45 cm (18 in), and *T. orientalis* 'Aurea Nana', 60 cm (2 ft) and 'Rosedalis', 60 cm (2 in).

There are many decorative shrubs and small trees which can contribute attractive foliage, flowers and, in some cases, fruit to the rock garden scene. They include the daphnes *Daphne cneorum* and *D. arbuscula,* height up to 15 cm (6 in); brooms *Cytisus ardoini,* 5—10 cm (2—4 in), *C. purpureus,* 60 cm (2 ft) and *Genista tinctoria* 'Humifusa', 7.5—10 cm (3—4 in); potentilla *Potentilla fruticosa* 'Tangerine', 60 cm (2 ft); dwarf China rose *Rosa chinensis* 'Minima', 30 cm (12 in); *Cotoneaster dammeri,* 5—10 cm (2—4 in), *C. congestus,* 5—15 cm (2—6 in), and *C. microphyllus,* 15 cm (6 in); *Berberis thunbergii* 'Atropurpurea Nana', 30—45 cm (12—18 in); rock roses *Cistus* x *corbariensis,* 90—120 cm (3—4 ft) and *C.* x *lusitanicus,* 30—60 cm (1—2 ft); spindle tree *Euonymus fortunei* 'Carrieri', 75—90 cm (2 $^1/_2$—3 ft).

Stunted China roses are among the smallest rockery roses.

Daphne arbuscula is one of the most beautiful small-leafed evergreen shrubs for the rockery.

84 Longer Life for Cut Flowers

Extending the vase life of cut flowers depends greatly on when they are cut and how long the flowers have been in bloom when they are cut. The ideal time to cut is early in the morning or late in the evening during warm and dry weather. For most species, cut half-opened flowers (though composite inflorescences such as those of China aster (*Callistephus chinensis*) and *Zinnia,* for instance, must be fully opened). Cut peonies (*Paeonia*) and day lily (*Hemerocallis*) at a stage when the buds are still closed but show their colour. Species with erect racemose inflorescences such as lupin (*Lupinus*) and *Delphinium,* should be cut when about one third or half of the flowers on the raceme have opened. Species whose flowers open only during sunny weather are not suitable for cutting; they include *Gazania,* cape marigold (*Dimorphotheca*), Californian poppy (*Eschscholtzia*), etc.

●

Cut the stems cleanly with a sharp knife. Remove any leaves on the stems which would be in water in the vase.

◀ With their shape, colour and long-lasting blooms, the small-flowered chrysanthemums (*C. indicum* varieties) are among the most suitable flowers for cutting.

Add fresh water to the vase every day and change it completely every two or three days. You can also buy special preparations to add to the water to extend the vase life of the flowers.

●

The life of cut flowers is shortened by direct sunlight, droughts, central heating and, surprisingly, by gases emitted by certain fruit, particularly apples, so do not place a vase with flowers next to a bowl of fruit. Some flowers, including roses, carnations, lily-of-the-valley, daffodils, lilies, sweet peas, mignonette (*Reseda*) and yellow primroses, release substances into the water which damage other cut flowers, so keep these flowers in a separate vase.

●

Cut flowers which last a particularly long time include perennials such as chrysanthemums, leopard's-bane (*Doronicum*), fleabane (*Erigeron*), *Gaillardia,* false sunflower (*Heliopsis*), *Leucanthemum maximum, Liatris,* peonies (*Paeonia*), coneflower (*Rudbeckia*), pincushion flower (*Scabiosa*) and *Tanacetum coccineum.* Long-lasting annuals and biennals include *Calendula,* China aster (*Callistephus*), bellflower (*Campanula*), cornflower (*Centaurea*), pink (*Dianthus caryophyllus*), sunflower (*Helianthus*), sweet pea (*Lathyrus odoratus*), stock (*Matthiola*), *Salpiglossis,* marigold (*Tagetes*) and *Zinnia.*

An attractive combination of flowers for a vase: Shasta daisy (*Chrysanthemum maximum*), blue delphiniums (*Delphinium elatum* varieties), red Maltese cross (*Lychnis chalcedonica*), and yellow *Lysimachia punctata.*

85 Containers for Cut Flowers

It is very important to choose a suitable vessel to make an arranged bouquet of flowers look attractive. When selecting a vessel ensure that the material, colour, shape and size harmonize with the flowers.

The vessel should, above all, be stable, keep the flowers firmly fixed and provide them with the necessary amount of water. Vases should have a simple shape and inconspicuous colour and decoration. White, black, grey, brown and green vases harmonize with most flower colours. Do not use vases that are too colourful or decorative or are of fanciful shape.

●

In general, the best vessels for simple flower forms as well as for richly colourful blooms are large ceramic vases. On the other hand, sprays of small-flowered, subtly coloured blooms look their best in vases made of cut glass, porcelain or other delicate materials. Field flowers and the inflorescences of decorative grasses look best in a dark ceramic jug. Place small flowers in

◀ A selection of flower-vases. Try to choose a vase that blends with the size, colour and character of the flowers.

An attractive arrangement of flowers in a vase.

small and shallow vessels, flowers on long leafless stems into tall glass or porcelain vases. Do not place stem-holding wire mesh in transparent vessels.

Bowls are now being used more and more for flowering arrangements. They can be of various materials — ceramics, porcelain, glass or metal — and of a size and shape to suit the particular subject. Flowers can be fixed to a bowl with the use of a kenzan (a metal needlepoint holder), a perforated ceramic or plastic lining, synthetic foam, or a moss cushion fixed to a bowl with wires. Fix the kenzan to the bottom of the bowl with glass cement so it does not move about; it can then be covered with moss.

Bowls. The centre drawings contain (left) a metal needlepoint holder (kenzan), and (right) a mossy cushion for flower arranging.

86 Flower Arranging Techniques

Dot not put too many flowers in a vase. Arrange the flowers irregularly in size so they are not all at the same level. Place smaller and lighter-coloured flowers in the top part of a bouquet with flowers of various size and colour, and darker and bigger flowers as well as foliage in the lower part of the bouquet.

Flowers stems should not be crossed over each other in a vase. The best way to arrange them is to stick the cut ends of the stems into plastic foam or into a ball of galvanized wire placed in the vase. The kenzan, or metal needlepoint holder, can also be used to fix the stems.

Flowers in a vase standing next to a wall need to be arranged only on the side facing into the room, whereas a bouquet placed in the middle of the table must look attractive from all sides. For traditional arrangements, use the principle of the 'golden cut': the height of the vase to the height of the flowers above the vase top should be in the ratio 3 : 5. The optimum width of the vase and of the bouquet is calculated in the same way. Modern flower arrangement is freer, although care must always be taken to achieve a visual balance between vase and flowers.

Flowers arranged in a bowl.

Bouquets tend to look best with a restricted range of colours. Warm colours (yellow, orange, red) have a cheerful effect; cool colours (blue, violet, green) create a more serious mood. To soften the effect of bouquets include plants with fine leaves such as ornamental *Asparagus,* or with tiny flowers like baby's breath (*Gypsophila*), *Astilbe,* coral bells (*Heuchera*), meadow rue (*Thalictrum*), etc.

Three basic lines — vertical, horizontal and slanting — are used for arranging flowers in bowls. Many harmonizing compositions can be created by combining the three. When arranging flowers, begin by placing those with the longest stems, fine shapes and bright colours in the middle. Position them into slanting lines. Place the larger, darker flowers as low as possible. The tallest flower and its stem should be about twice as long as the length or diameter of the bowl. Place the small branches of woody plants or flowers of natural drooping growth in a horizontal position. A bowl arranged with flowers in such a way should give the impression that all the flowers are emerging from one point.

Flowers in a clay jug.

87 Plants Dangerous to Health

It's not always realised that many decorative plants grown in the garden are poisonous. One of the most dangerous is monkshood (*Aconitum napellus*), which was used as a poison in medieval times. This perennial and its many fine cultivars, with their interesting dark-blue flowers, is widely grown. In view of the fact that every part of the plant is poisonous, it should never be used as a cut flower.

●

Among the most dangerous of plants are those with decorative but poisonous fruits, which children may mistake for edible garden fruit. Typical of these is mezereon (*Daphne mezereum*), which bears attractive scarlet berries. Children need to be

◄ Monkshood (*Aconitum*) is one of the most poisonous plants in all its parts.

taught about the danger of some plants as soon as possible. Of those perennials flowering in early spring, hellebores (*Helleborus*) and *Adonis vernalis,* with yellow flowers, are dangerous. Of the autumn perennials, the lilac-flowered *Colchicum autumnale* is highly poisonous, as is *Cyclamen purpurascens* with its beautiful carmine flowers. Among the most poisonous decorative plants is the foxglove (*Digitalis purpurea*), whose leaves are used for making a powerful drug to treat heart diseases. *Paeonia officinalis* also causes undesirable effects, while the male fern (*Dryopteris filix-mas*) and its rhizomes are dangerous for people suffering from heart disease.

The fruits of certain decorative woody plants are poisonous in varying degrees. These include *Laburnum,* evergreen privet (*Ligustrum*), *Viburnum,* common ivy (*Hedera helix*), and spindle tree (*Euonymus*).

Some flowers cause rashes in people with sensitive skin. Among these are certain species of cowlips. Even worse is the beautiful but dangerous burning bush (*Dictamnus albus*): the entire plant, especially its capsuled fruit, is covered in stinging glands containing a strong-smelling essential oil which causes inflammation of the skin. Always cut off the wilted flowers of this plant with gloves and never handle any part of it with bare hands.

Poisonous flowers in the garden: (a) *Adonis,* (b) autumn crocus (*Colchicum*), (c) foxglove (*Digitalis*), (d) lily-of-the-valley (*Convallaria majalis*), (e) mezereon (*Daphne mezereum*), (f) hellebore (*Helleborus*), (g) *Cyclamen.*

88 Changing Your Garden Layout

Even the best laid-out decorative garden needs constant alteration and adjustment. The location and arrangement of annuals and biennials, depending on the species, should be changed annually. Certain bulbous and tuberous flowers, including tulips, hyacinths and gladioli, should be located in a different site every year. Perennials can remain on one site for different lengths of time. When they begin to lack vitality and their flowers deteriorate, they should have their crowns divided and be transplanted to a new site with well-prepared, fertile soil.

●

The most stable part of a decorative garden is the rockery. Since its construction and planting is expensive in both money and physical effort, its basic structure and shape should be regarded as permanent. However, it often happens that some plants, for reasons difficult to fathom, grow reluctantly in what should have been a suitable site. They then have to be transplanted elsewhere on the rockery or a border and replaced with a more suitable species.

Proceed carefully and sensitively when carrying out adjustments and alterations in a decorative garden. Try to harmonize the natural requirements of individual plants with your desire to make the garden attractive in your particular way. Try to understand the needs and preferences of each individual variety of plant you wish to use. Much knowledge and insight can be acquired by visiting public gardens and botanical parks. They may help inspire you to make the best and most exciting use of your own plot.

Water-lily tulip (*Tulipa kaufmanniana* 'Corona') in the area in front of a rockery.

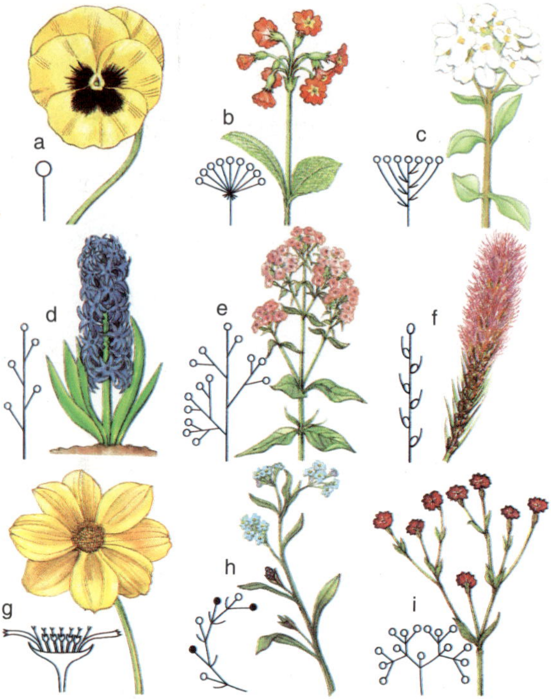

The commonest forms of flowers on decorative herbaceous plants: (a) single flower (garden pansy, *Viola* x *wittrockiana*); (b) an umbel (primrose, *Primula rosea*); (c) corymb, or flat-topped cluster of flowers (*Iberis*); (d) raceme, or unbranched spirally arranged flower-head (hyacinth, *Hyacinthus*); (e) panicle, or large branched flower cluster (*Phlox*); (f) spike, or unbranched head of stalkless flowers (*Liatris*); (g) large single flower (*Dahlia*); (h) monochasium, or a flower-head that produces only one main axis (forget-me-not, *Myosotis*); (i) dichasium, or a flower-head that produces two main axes (rose campion, *Lychnis coronaria*).

Common types of inflorescence in ornamental plants

The shapes of most of the inflorescences of individual species are described in the text. Some of the most important ones are shown in the above pictures.

More flowers suitable for the garden

Name	Height cm	Flowers in month	Inflorescence, shape, colour	Comment
Perennials				
Acanthus hungaricus – Acanthus	80–100	7	spike, p	△
Aethionema grandiflorum – Stone cress	20–25	5–6	raceme, p	+Ca
Ajuga reptans – Bugleweed	10–15	5–6	verticillaster, b, w	○ ◑
Artemisia nitida – Tarragon	10–15	7–8	raceme of anthodiums, yg	+Ca

Dodecatheon meadia – Common shooting-star	30–40	5–6	umbel, p, w	◑ Hu +Ca dies back after flowering
Eriogonum umbellatum – Eriogonum	12–20	5–6	umbel, y	
Eryngium alpinum – Alpine eryngo	60–80	7–8	capitulum, gb	∵
Geum x *hybridum* – Avens hybrids	25–50	5–6	corymb, y, o, r	▭ ∵ Hu
Globularia cordifolia – Globe daisy	6–7	5–6	capitulum, bv	Hu +Ca
Haberlea rhodopensis – Haberlea	10–15	5–6	raceme, bv	◑ ● Hu +Ca
Jasione laevis – Sheep's bit	20–30	6–8	capitulum, bv	+Ca
Kniphofia x *hybrida* – Red-hot poker	70–100	7–8	raceme, y, o, r	∵
Malva moschata – Musk mallow	30–60	6–7	raceme, p	○ ◑ ∵
Potentilla nitida – Cinquefoil	5	7–8	individual, p	
Ramonda myconi – Ramonda	8–10	5–6	individual, v, w, p	◑ ● Hu +Ca
Scabiosa caucasica – Pincushion flower	50–80	7–9	capitulum bv, w	∵ Hu +Ca
Soldanella montana – Snowbell	10–15	4–5	individual, bv	◑ Hu −Ca
Solidago x *hybrida* – Goldenrod	60–100	7–9	panicles of anthodiums, y	▭ ∵ ✂
Tradescantia x *andersoniana* – Spiderwort	40–60	7–9	corymb, b, w, r	○ ◑ ▭ ∵
Viola cornuta – Pansy	10–20	5–9	individual, b, v, y, p	Hu

Annuals

Amaranthus caudatus – Love-lies-bleeding	60–120	7–10	drooping spike, r	Hu +Ca △ ∵
Celosia argentea cristata – Cockscomb	25–50	7–9	comb, panicles, y, r	Hu ▭ ∵
Cosmos sulphureus – Cosmea, or cosmos	70–90	6–10	anthodium, y, o	▭ ✂
Eschscholtzia californica – Californian poppy	30–40	7–8	individual, w, r, o	▭
Helianthus annuus – Sunflower	100–130	7–9	anthodium, y	Hu △ ∵

Iberis umbellata – Candytuft	25–30	6–7	corymb, w, p, r	□ [little watering]
Kochia scoparia – Summer cypress	80–100		inconspicuous	low hedgerows, △
Salpiglossis sinuata – Painted tongue	50–80	7–8	raceme, p	□ ✂ [little watering]
Schizanthus x *wisetonensis* – Butterfly flower	40	7–8	raceme, colourful	Hu [little watering] □ ✂
Tropaeolum majus – Nasturtium	35	7–10	individual, r, o, y	□ [decorative pot]

Bulbous and tuberous flowers

Anemone coronaria – Poppy anemone	25–35	5–7	individual, w, r, b, v	□ ⁖ ✂ [winter cover]
Camassia quamash – Camass, or quamash	35–50	5–6	raceme, b	Hu □ ⁖ ✂
Chionodoxa luciliae – Glory-of-the-snow	12–15	3–4	raceme, b + w	◑ Hu ⁖ [rockery]
Galtonia candicans – Summer hyacinth	80–120	7–8	raceme, w	⁖ △ ✂
Iris x *hollandica* – Dutch iris	40–50	6–7	individual, w, y, b	□ ⁖ ✂
Iridodictyum reticulatum	10–15	3	individual, v, b	[rockery] [winter cover]
Oxalis deppei – Sorrel	15–20	7–9	umbel, p	◑ Hu $^{-}$Ca ⁖ [rockery]
Tigridia pavonia – Tiger flower	40–50	7–9	individual, colourful	Hu □ ⁖

Explanations for the signs:

- ○ sunny site
- ◑ semi-shaded site
- ● shaded site
- □ plantation in a bed
- ⁖ plantation in a clump
- △ plantation as a solitary plant
- [rockery] plantation in a rockery
- [decorative pot] plantation in a decorative pot

- Hu humus-rich soil
- [little watering] little watering
- [decorative flower foliage] decorative flower foliage
- ✂ flower suitable for cutting
- $^{+}$Ca requires calcium in soil
- $^{-}$Ca does not tolerate calcium in soil
- [winter cover] requires a winter cover

Colour of inflorescence:

- w white
- y yellow
- p pink
- r red
- b blue
- v violet
- o orange
- g grey

Index of Common Names

Figures refer to hint numbers, T indicates table on pp. 186-188.

Index of Botanical Names